THE DAY THAT
DERBY
WON THE CUP

THE DAY THAT DERBY WON THE CUP

ANTON RIPPON

NORTH BRIDGE PUBLISHING

First published in Great Britain in 2014 by
North Bridge Publishing
20 Chain Lane
Mickleover
Derby DE3 9AJ

ISBN 978-0-9926779-3-0

Book design by Graham Hales, Derby

Printed and bound by CMP (UK) Ltd, Dorset

Contents

Introduction

On 30 April 1946 I was in St Peter's Street, Derby, perched on the outer wall of the church that gave its name to that part of the north-south spine which runs through the city – it was then just a town, of course – waiting for Derby County to come past with the FA Cup. Or at least I am led to believe that I was there. I was only 16 months old at the time and have no recollection of the occasion. I have only my late mother's word for it. True, a picture is indelibly imprinted on my mind, but it is one almost certainly conjured up from photographs of the occasion, images that I saw much later.

But I'm sure that I was there and for that I will be eternally grateful to my mother for thinking that, years later, her infant son might like to say: "I was there when Derby County brought home the FA Cup." And I have said it, many times, because it was a moment that, 68 years later, has yet to be repeated.

My first visit to the Baseball Ground was in December 1952, on my eighth birthday. Two members of the 1946 FA Cup-winning team were playing that day – Chick Musson and Jack Stamps. I later saw another – Reg Harrison – play for the Rams. Ten years later, I even managed to play against Stamps and Harrison in charity matches. Both became friends. Jack invited me to his golden wedding anniversary, Reg to his birthday celebrations.

In 1984, then working for BBC Radio Derby, I interviewed seven of the 1946 Cup-winning team: Jack and Reg, obviously, and also Jack Howe, Jimmy Bullions, Raich Carter, Peter Doherty and Dally Duncan. By then, Vic Woodley, Jack Nicholas, Leon Leuty and Chick Musson had passed away, the latter two at an unbelievably cruel young age, both still in their mid-30s.

In the spring of 2014, only Reg and Jimmy are still with us. The "babies" of the 1946 "Veterans' Final now themselves both 90 years of age.

The Day That Derby Won The Cup has thus long been an important day for me. And, without doubt, for thousands more Derby County fans too, whether they were lucky enough to be at Wembley on that warm spring day in 1946, whether they were born years later. Or whether, like me, someone took the trouble to lift them up to see the Cup come home.

What follows in an account, not just of that special day, but of the whole season as the first FA Cup competition of the post-war period unfolded.

Anton Rippon
Derby
Spring, 2014

Preface

DENNIS Chambers opened his eyes, shifted his legs and looked out of the carriage window. For the hundredth time in three quarters of an hour he wondered what the score was.

Then he closed his eyes again and re-imposed the scene upon his imagination: one team in white shirts, the other in red. The whites were on the attack. The ball was swung out to the right wing and returned almost immediately. A head rose above all other heads and nodded towards goal. Then the net bulged.

Dennis lifted himself ever so slightly off his seat. But before he could conjure up the celebrations that would surely have followed his version of events, he was jolted back to the present by the noise of the door sliding open. The ticket inspector had pushed his way into the crowded compartment and was already clipping holes in small bits of coloured cardboard and peering at crumpled travel warrants.

"How's Derby doing, mate?" Dennis enquired, more in hope than expectation that the fussy little man might be interested in football.

"Derby? It was there when we left this morning."

"No, I mean the Cup Final."

"Cup Final? I thought they scrubbed that sort of thing when there was a war on."

"Well, there isn't a war on, is there?" Dennis snapped back. "Not any more."

The ticket inspector adopted a mocking tone: "Where've you been anyway?"

"Africa, mate," Dennis shot back. "Bloody Africa. Then Greece."

The man decided that he wasn't going to win what he'd meant as a bit of banter but which had quickly developed a sharp edge.

"Fair enough, mate," he said, stepping backwards into the corridor and sliding shut the compartment door without bothering to check Dennis's own travel documents.

"You been in Africa, then?"

Dennis looked across at the airman who'd been dozing opposite him since they left St Pancras, and who, up until now, hadn't said a word as they rattled north.

"Yeah," Dennis replied. With no further information forthcoming, the airman closed his eyes again. Everyone else stared straight ahead or out of the window.

Dennis looked at his watch. It was a quarter to four. Half-time. He was beginning to wish that he'd missed the train and instead found a pub with a wireless. Or, better still, after he'd arrived at Waterloo, actually gone to Wembley. He wouldn't have got in, but he would still have been there. Now he was on a slow train somewhere, probably in the middle of Northamptonshire. Wherever, he might as well have been a million miles from the FA Cup Final.

Anyway, it was half-time now. Dennis forgot about the football match for a moment and turned his mind to what lay ahead. It had been five years since he'd sat in the Marquis of Granby and wondered if the Coulson twins would ever give up the dartboard. And even longer – seven years – since he'd last walked down to the Baseball Ground and pushed his way through a turnstile and on to the terrace behind the Osmaston goal. His mind went back to that uncomfortably sticky September Saturday. The previous day, Germany had invaded Poland. Then Derby had beaten Aston Villa and he'd had a grandstand view of the winning goal, a penalty scored by Jack Nicholas, low and hard to the goalkeeper's right hand.

It would be a long time before Derby scored another. That evening there was a thunderstorm and someone said that a barrage balloon over Rolls-Royce had been struck by lightning. The following day, Dennis had just been getting ready to stroll over to the Marquis when Neville Chamberlain told everyone that the country was at war. He went to the Marquis anyway. The Coulsons were still hogging the dartboard, but this time it didn't seem to matter. Someone tried a joke: the Prime Minister had said that the Government had no option but to declare war. Fair enough, but why drag us all in? No-one laughed. On the Monday, Dennis had gone straight down to the Assembly Rooms and joined up.

Now it was all over, he was coming home, and Derby County were playing in the FA Cup Final.

When he'd gone to the Assembly Rooms on that Monday morning in the late summer of 1939, Dennis had just celebrated his 19th birthday. He'd not even bothered to tell his boss that he would be late for work that day. Derby Town Council's wages department had never appealed to him. He'd applied only because his parents suggested it when he was about to leave Bemrose School. They'd seen the job advertised in the *Derby Evening Telegraph*.

"You'll have a job for life, son," his father had told him. Dennis had soon realised that he didn't want a job for life. At least not one that involved working out the wages of dustmen, school caretakers and dinner ladies. Joining up seemed a reasonable escape route.

For two years the Army had him moved around the country and, some weekends, he'd even managed to get home and sleep in his own bed. By then, some of the big clubs had started playing football again but Derby County wasn't one of them. So, on his rare Saturdays back in Derby, Dennis had caught a bus to the Municipal Sports Ground and watched some of the Derby players turn out for the Carriage and Wagon team. The standard wasn't all that good, but it was still a game of football.

He was coming up for his 21st birthday when the Army sent him abroad. He'd just had time to marry Beryl, then the whole family – both families, actually – had come down to see him off at the LMS Station. Two days later he was leaning on the rails of the troopship *Duchess of Bedford* as she slipped anchor, and he watched Liverpool's skyline disappear. Then it was all a blur: Algeria for a few months, then the invasion of Sicily, then Greece. After four years away, the Army gave him a month's leave, in theory ample time to get home to see Beryl and Tommy, who'd just started school. Dennis had never seen Tommy. But, somehow, he never got further than Italy before his leave ran out.

He had, though, managed to keep in touch with Derby County's doings. They'd reached the Cup semi-finals before the Army finally let him go in the early spring of 1946, and he'd harboured hopes of getting home, buying a ticket, and going to Wembley. It had been an over-ambitious plan. It took him four days to get to Sorrento on a ship, two weeks on a train to Calais, then a ferry to Dover, then another train to Catterick, and he was finally demobbed somewhere in Surrey. Why the Army couldn't have waved him goodbye in North Yorkshire, he didn't know. Why they had to send him all the way back down south was a puzzle. But after five years of service life, Dennis was used to puzzles. Nothing much ever made sense. It was just his bloody luck, though, a supreme irony, that he'd finally collected his demob suit and a travel warrant back to Derby on the very day that half the town seemed to be coming the other way.

Dennis looked out of the carriage window again and considered his dilemma once more: how could he walk into the house, look at the wife he'd not seen for five years, and at a son he'd never met, and, before he asked anyone how they were, enquire what the score was at Wembley?

Teething Problems

ON 15 August 1945, Great Britain celebrated the end of the Second World War. In Derby, as everywhere, there were street parties, lots of them. In Rivett Street, 30 children enjoyed homemade cakes and buns. The major feature of the party in Melbourne Street was a 7lbs iced "Victory Peace Cake" made by Mrs Ethel Wright. In King Alfred Street old-age pensioners were invited to a children's party and enjoyed fruit, jelly, cakes and buns. In Goodwin Street, 161 happy faces testified to the quality of the fare bought by the £9 5s 0d collected for the occasion, while children in Offerton Avenue burned an effigy of the Japanese warlord, Togo, and the anti-aircraft battery on Kingsway loaned their canteen so that the children of the Westleigh Estate could stage their party.

On Chester Green there was a football match between local men and women who swapped clothes for the occasion. At St James's Road School, the problem of finding enough fat to bake cakes was solved when Mrs H. Rawlings went round the neighbourhood to beg a piece of margarine "the size of a walnut" from each resident. Soon she had enough to begin work.

In the Market Place, thousands danced to the accompaniment of the Rolls-Royce Band, which competed with several impromptu "orchestras" around the square. At midnight, a huge crowd sang *Abide With Me* before falling into a two-minute silence to remember the dead. Six long, war weary years were finally over. Now the nation could attempt to rebuild their lives and to return to normality, whatever that was.

Of course, there was nothing more normal than football, and the following day, 16 August, Derby County and Nottingham Forest played each other in a VJ Day celebration match in front of an 8,000 holiday crowd at the City Ground. Three months earlier the teams had staged a similar match at the Baseball Ground to celebrate VE Day. That was a 2-2 draw but, this time, the Rams ran out easy winners against their local rivals. It was a game played "in a peace-loving manner" according to the *Derby Evening Telegraph's* "Mark Eaton" who remarked that, had their been points at stake, "the Rams would most probably have reached double-figures".

Derby led 2-1 at half-time, through Raich Carter and Dally Duncan, and Ted Attwood, a centre-forward who had been impressing after signing from Markeaton Rangers, added two goals in the second half to make the final score 4-1. "Young

Watson," a 17-year-old goalkeeper from Shelton United had also impressed, it seems.

Nine days later, the final football season of the Second World War kicked-off on 25 August 1945 (officially the war still had a few days to run because the Japanese would not surrender with a signed document until 2 September, but the dropping of atomic bombs on the cities of Hiroshima and Nagasaki had already signalled the end). Britain also had a new prime minister. In July, Labour had been swept to power with an overwhelming majority for the first time in the party's history. The nation that had revered Winston Churchill as its wartime leader rejected him for its peacetime prosperity.

Many of the country's professional footballers, in dispute with their employers, had voted for Clement Attlee. On the eve of the new season they read of Attlee's warning to the country: peace had heralded not days of plenty but even greater austerity. The abrupt ending of Lease-Lend by the US Government meant major cuts in imports, while goods meant for home consumption would now have to be exported. There were hard times ahead. On a brighter note, after more than 2,000 nights of blackout, the lights had been switched on again, although midwinter football matches would still have to kick-off early; floodlighting was still some years away. It was announced that in December, one million servicemen would be demobbed; a million people would also be released from munitions work. Some of them would be footballers, back in the only full-time employment they had ever wanted.

As football strived for normality, everyone knew that it would be not be easy to shake off the effects of the war. Writing in the *Athletic News Football Annual*, Ivan Sharpe, a famous amateur international of the pre-First World War era who numbered Derby County among his club, had warned as much: "This is the seventh season of emergency football – a period more protracted than expected and teeming with problems for clubs and players. The only advances on last season are that the full list of international matches is resumed and that the FA Cup competition returns, though the Cup change is a gain more in name than in fact to the main body of competitors – the professional clubs – whose Football League War Cups have been highly popular."

As they had been prone to do throughout wartime, when the Football League put forward plans for the 1945-46 season, many clubs had objected. The League wanted to revert to the set-up which had been abandoned in 1939: First, Second and Third Divisions North and South. The only concession was that there would be no promotion and relegation. Clubs would have a full season in which to settle down before the serious business resumed. The full member clubs – those in the First and Second Divisions – disagreed, albeit only by a small majority. They wanted to divide themselves into two groups, north and south, although they were prepared to let their lesser brethren, the associate members who made up the Third Divisions, return to their pre-war format immediately. The minnows also railed against this and the northern and southern sections were each further divided into two sections, so there were the confusing Third Division South (South) and Third Division South (North), and the Third Division North (West) and Third Division North (East). The new Third Division sections were agreed barely a month before the beginning of the season and the fixtures had to be hurriedly rearranged. The only absentees were Hull City and New Brighton, both of whom were in the midst of reorganisation and moving grounds. Guest players would be restricted to six per team with the hope that this could be reduced as soon as possible.

Clubs, both big and small, argued that the shortage of players and the difficulties of travel and finding hotel accommodation had not been sufficiently eased. Their case was underlined as early as 12 September 1945, when, under the headline "It's A Nightmare For Soccer Managers", the *Daily Mail* reported: "There has been a lot of head scratching by harassed football club managers over the heavy League programme ... Almost every manager has a story to tell of borrowing and making-do .... They have had to beg to secure the release of their men in the forces ... Then there is the travel problem. The luxury motor coaches in which teams travelled the country in 1939 have gone; trains are fewer. It is a good thing that there is no trip like the 480 miles Derby County had to cover last week to play Plymouth ... 480 miles these days, when it is impossible to reserve train accommodation, and even the corridors are packed, is no joke for any team."

The Derby County team that beat Nottingham Forest 5-0 in a Football League North match at the Baseball Ground in September 1944: back row (left to right): John Marshall, Reg Trim, Jimmy Bullions, Ray Bilton, Leon Leuty, Chick Musson. Front row: Peter Doherty, Sammy Crooks, Fred Tapping, Tommy Powell, Dally Duncan.

The Rams' forward line for their Football League South match against West Bromwich Albion at the Baseball Ground in December 1945: from left to right: Reg Harrison, Raich Carter, Dave McCulloch, Peter Doherty, Dally Duncan. Harrison, Carter and McCulloch scored in a 3-3 draw.

The Rams side that lost 3-1 at Coventry City in a Football League South game in March 1946, a few days after reaching the FA Cup semi-final: back row (left to right): Dave Willis (trainer), Jimmy Bullions, Jack Parr, Vic Woodley, Angus Morrison, Chick Musson, Dally Duncan. Front row: Reg Harrison, Raich Carter, Leon Leuty, Jack Nicholas, Peter Doherty, John Shearer.

The bomb-damaged Osmaston Stand at the Baseball Ground, hit during a German air-raid in January 1941.

Wartime Football

WHEN war had been declared in September 1939, football – indeed, all sport – had closed down immediately. The Football League programme had been only three games old when the blackout went up. Derby County had started with a 3-0 defeat at Sunderland before beating Portsmouth, the FA Cup holders, 2-0 at the Baseball Ground in midweek and then, on the final Saturday of peace, Aston Villa 1-0, also at home. There had been barely 8,000 spectators scattered around the Baseball Ground on the sultry afternoon. As they drifted out into the streets of Pear Tree, few had bothered to discuss the match they had just seen. They already knew that it would count for nothing.

The reaction of football's rulers had been not to make the same mistake as in 1914 when the Football League and the

FA Cup had been allowed to continue for a whole season and everyone connected with the game had been denounced as both unpatriotic and unproductive. In November 1914, *The Times* had carried a letter from the historian A. H. Pollard: " ... Every club that employs a professional football player is bribing a much-needed recruit away from enlistment and every spectator who pays his gate money is contributing so much towards a German victory." The FA had responded by claiming that 500,000 recruits had already been raised by football organisations, that of 5,000 professionals, some 2,000 were already in the services, and only 600 unmarried professional footballers had failed to heed the call.

Of course, there were fundamental differences between 1914 and 1939. Volunteer soldiers had fought the early months of the First World War. Conscription, introduced in 1939, had prevented a repeat of that. And there had been the imminent threat of air attack. By 1939, the prospect of German air-raids on British cities had been in the public mind for several years. Thus, one of the Government's first reactions after the declaration of war had been to ban the assembly of crowds. That meant that all forms of public entertainment had to be suspended immediately. The *Daily Mail* of 4 September 1939 had commented: "For the moment, all sport has been brought to a halt. The concentration of Britain's whole effort on winning the war makes its continuance undesired and inappropriate."

So, unlike 1914, in 1939 football had had no choice to make; the game could not carry on anyway. On 5 September, the Football League had told its member clubs to keep their players on stand-by. Then, after a hastily arranged meeting at Crewe, the League had further informed clubs to release the players after all, paying them up to 6 September. Bonuses and any other additional payments should be settled at once, supporters would have to wait until it was decided what to do about refunding money for season tickets, and if the regular season could be resumed later, matches already played would count as cup games. Thus football had hung in limbo until, a few days after war had been declared, then the Government had lifted its ban on sporting activities outside highly populated areas such as London, Birmingham and Manchester.

Soon, the areas where matches could be played had been extended provided that local police did not object. The first friendlies when spectators could be admitted had taken place on 16 September with 28 matches involving Football League teams in England and three games in Scotland. Attendances had ranged from 2,000 to 9,000, and altogether totalled 117,000. Derby County had not played that day, but when they did give it a go, on 30 September, only 1,805 people had turned up at the Baseball Ground for a friendly game against Leeds United. That was enough to convince the Derby directors to shut up shop.

The Baseball Ground had been handed over to the military and Derby County's pre-war players, whether they were now in the armed forces, the police or Civil Defence, or working in munitions factories, had gone off to play for other clubs. It would be Christmas Day 1941 before what could be considered a Derby County first team played again. That day they lost 3-1 to an RAF XI at the Baseball Ground where 10,000 sports-starved supporters saw a 16-year-old

Bemrose School pupil called Tommy Powell take his place in a forward line that also included pre-war stars Sammy Crooks, Jack Bowers, Peter Ramage and Dally Duncan.

By the end of the season the Rams had played several friendly matches against an eclectic round of opposition, such as the Czechoslovakian Armed Forces, the Belgian Army, Anti-Aircraft Command, the Pick of the Derby and District Senior League and Birmingham (they had still to add "City"). Attendances had generally been around the 10,000 mark and those fans had seen an equally eclectic selection of players in Derby shirts, ranging from former England men like Crooks and Bowers to raw youngsters spotted while playing on Derby's public parks.

Nevertheless, those five-figure attendance figures had encouraged the Derby board to enter wartime regional football proper for 1942-43. When the war leagues had started, it had been decided that players would be paid 30 shillings (£1.50) as opposed to the maximum pre-war weekly wage of £8. Guest players would be allowed, provided the player's original club granted permission.

The make-up of the wartime Football League and the weekly progress of its clubs had taken some following. Derby County had entered the Football League North, which had meant a "first period" of 18 league matches up to Christmas. After Christmas, a War Cup had begun with the northern and southern sections then combining in a qualifying competition where each club had played against five others on a home and away basis, these small pools having been selected by the Football League. All the cup games had also counted towards the championship's "second period", and the top 32 teams had then gone into a straightforward knockout competition with extra league matches making up the "second championship". Clubs played no more than 20 matches each. Those playing fewer had had their points calculated on the average they would have won had they played 20 games. Pocket calculators were more than a generation away. Supporters had to brush up their arithmetic, or simply wait for the newspapers to publish league tables.

The Rams had finished 9th and 18th in the "first" and "second" championships respectively, and lost 5-3 on aggregate to Notts County in the first round of the War Cup knockout competition. In 1943-44, Derby had been 19th and 23rd, and knocked out of the War Cup by Coventry City, and of the Midland Cup by Stoke City. By 1944-45, however, the Rams' fortunes shifted dramatically. They had finished runners-up before winning the "second" championship. And they had won the Midland Cup by beating Aston Villa, 9-0 on aggregate in the Final. The difference was a full-time manager, Ted Magner, who had managed to fashion a team out of guest players and youngsters. One of guests, Raich Carter, had scored a hat-trick at Villa Park. Another Derby guest, Peter Doherty, had netted five against Villa at the Baseball Ground. Derby County fans were going to hear a lot more of Raich Carter and Peter Doherty, especially when it came to cup football.

Carter and Doherty

O N the morning of Friday, 21 December 1945, Raich Carter was walking out his camp at RAF Loughborough, looking forward to 14 days' leave with his wife and baby daughter in Derby, when a fellow airman caught him up and delivered a message that Carter had to meet the directors of Derby County Football Club at a hotel in the town as soon as possible. Carter knew what it was about. He had been a guest player for the Rams since October 1943, marking his first game in a Derby shirt with a hat-trick from inside-forward against Birmingham at the Baseball Ground that same month.

Carter had been posted from RAF Innsworth Lane in Gloucestershire to Loughborough, where he helped to rehabilitate injured airman. It had been what he desperately wanted. A German bomb had destroyed his home in Sunderland – his England caps had gone with it – and his wife and child were living with his in-laws at Chaddesden, on the outskirts of Derby. Getting a posting to Loughborough meant that he could over to see his family much more easily than from deepest Gloucestershire. Happily for Derby County, it also meant that he could play for the Rams.

Before the war, before he was even 21 in fact, Carter had won every top honour then available to an English footballer – full international caps, Football League championship winners' medal, FA Cup winners' medal, all with his native Sunderland. But he no longer had family ties with the town, and he had fallen out with its football club. Carter had asked for an accrued share of his benefit – his second one – up to September 1939, and, now that the war was over, a ten-year contract with the Wearsiders. The club responded by placing him on the transfer list. That was enough for the proud Carter. Remaining with Derby County would suit him very well indeed.

At the Derby hotel, Carter learned that negotiations for his transfer were almost complete. The Rams were simply awaiting a telephone call from Sunderland. The problem was that midnight on that day was zero hour if the Rams wanted Carter to play for them in the FA Cup, two weeks hence. And, of course, they did. So while the Derby officials waited for the phone, Carter and the Derby secretary, Jack Catterall, set off by train for Sunderland. They reached their change at York at 8pm, whereupon Catterall found a telephone box, rang Derby, and was delighted to be told to go on to Sunderland. Everything had been settled. The fee would be £6,000

("Derby were lucky to get me for that, and Sunderland were silly to sell me for that," the player said later) and it was full steam ahead.

But there was a problem. The combination of what were still effectively wartime travel conditions, and people trying to get home for Christmas, meant that Carter and Catterall could not get anywhere near the Sunderland train on a crowded platform. They saw it pull out of York, leaving them stranded. Catterall rushed out into the station yard and began bargaining with taxi drivers. Eventually he found one who had enough petrol – again these were difficult times – and they raced through the late evening, reaching Sunderland, 70 miles away, with an hour to spare. The Sunderland officials were waiting for them at the Grand Hotel, the forms were signed, and Raich Carter was a Rams guest player no more. Now he was official.

In September 1944, Carter had scored four goals for the Combined Services XI against Ireland. His side won 8-4 and Peter Doherty, a flame-haired Irish inside-forward who in the 1930s had danced his way through English football with Manchester City, scored all the Irish goals. Now, though, along with Raich Carter, Doherty was also guesting for Derby County. The pair had found themselves working together at No.3 Medical Rehabilitation Unit, RAF Loughborough, and it was only natural that Doherty should also turn out for the Rams, who each week provided seats for injured airmen to watch matches at the Baseball Ground.

Just as Carter was falling out with Sunderland, so Doherty was falling out with Manchester City who had shown an uncompromising and sometimes strange attitude about where

Doherty might guest. Once he promised to play for Walsall, but for some reason that he could not fathom City had insisted that he turn out for West Brom. When he told them that he wished to play for Derby County, City instead insisted that he play for, of all people, Manchester United. It did not make sense to the player who saw employers who simply wanted to stand in his way.

Relations between Doherty and City became strained beyond the point of reconciliation. Several possible moves were mooted, but by now the club had granted Doherty permission to guest for Derby and he had made his debut in a goalless draw at Nottingham Forest in the opening match of the 1944-45 season. And so in December 1945, he, too, signed for Derby County, and for the same fee as had Raich Cater – £6,000 – but without the attendant drama of a late-night taxi dash.

By the end of his first season as a Derby guest, Doherty had scored 35 goals in 29 matches, including those five against Aston Villa in the Midland Cup Final. Carter had 29 in 28 matches that season, to add to the 13 he had scored in only 14 appearances the previous season. Aston Villa had reportedly once offered Sunderland £8,000 for Carter, while Liverpool had once valued Doherty at £15,000 which Manchester City had turned down. Altogether, it was going to be £12,000 well spent by Derby County.

Ted Magner

WHEN the Rams started up again in 1941 it had been largely with the help of two pre-war players, Jack Nicholas and Jack Webb. Times were difficult for football clubs, as Nicholas, in particular, discovered. On one occasion the vagaries of wartime travel left goalkeeper Frank Boulton stranded in Birmingham. The reserve-team goalkeeper, Vanham, was summoned but he arrived at Derby Bus Station a few minutes after the Rams' team bus had left for Barnsley. So Nicholas found himself keeping goal. He let in only two, but the Rams, shorn of several first-teamers, didn't score any. Such were the problems of wartime football.

Towards the end of the 1943-44 season Derby County had a new full-time manager. It was their first such appointment since George Jobey had arrived at the Baseball Ground in the summer of 1925. When the Rams had re-formed, Jobey was not in a position to pick up the reins again. At the Midland

Hotel, Derby, in 1941, a joint FA-Football League commission had found him and several directors guilty of paying illegal wages and bonuses to Rams players throughout the 1930s. Jobey's punishment was a *sine die* suspension from all football. This was lifted in 1945, but by then the Rams were on their way to winning the FA Cup. And it was Ted Magner who set them on the road to Wembley.

Magner was 51 years old when the Rams approached him. Born in Newcastle upon Tyne, his playing career had been spent with Gainsborough Trinity, then a Second Division club, Everton and St Mirren. His second appearance in the Football League had been against the Rams, and he had also played at the Baseball Ground for Everton in the FA Cup in 1911. In 1913, for St Mirren he scored five in a game, against Queen's Park to set a Scottish First Division record.

But it was as a coach that Magner had made his name. After the First World War he had worked with clubs in Amsterdam. From 1935 to 1937 he had coached Olympique Lillois, guiding them to runners-up in the *Championnat de France* in 1936. In 1937 he moved to FC Metz, a young club that had just won promotion to the top flight of French football. Magner was always looking for a new challenge, however, and in 1939, he managed the Danish national team for the two-match tournament that celebrated the 50th anniversary of the Danish Football Association. Magner had introduced a level of fitness training hitherto unknown among the strictly amateur Danish players who, after losing 2-0 to Germany in a friendly, went on to win both their tournament matches, against Finland and Norway, 5-0 and 6-3 respectively in Copenhagen.

Magner had then returned to Britain to coach the famous amateur club, Corinthians, and he had also become one of the most prominent members of the FA Scheme for Coaching, working as a tutor on refresher courses at Loughborough and Leeds.

In December 1938, he had been appointed Huddersfield Town's first-ever specialist coach, assisting manager Clem Stephenson, and from June 1942 he'd acted as Huddersfield's caretaker manager before David Steele, a member of the Town team that had won three Football League championships on the trot in the 1920s, took over, whereupon Magner had reverted to his original role of first-team coach. Then on 1 March 1944, he took over as Derby County's new manager.

Magner's first week at the Baseball Ground saw him on the pitch, in a tracksuit, coaching a crowd of young hopefuls. The *Derby Evening Telegraph* reported: "For an hour and a half last evening he was on the Baseball Ground with the young players, giving them tuition on dribbling, passing, trapping and shooting, while the more experienced men concentrated on keep-fit exercises. There was an unusually high concentration of players for this training-cum-coaching session. In fact it almost like 'old times' to see so many players at the ground other than on a match day."

Magner announced that during the summer he wanted to put into operation an extensive coaching scheme for youngsters, an integral part of which he hoped would be a Derby County Invitation Cup competition for players up to the age of 18. He joined the committee of the Derby and District Boys' Sports Association. He wanted to be involved, not just with Derby County's first team but also with any aspect that could help the club.

Peter Doherty could not speak too highly of Magner: "He was outstanding. His man-management was superb and he had an immense knowledge of the game. He could also play. He would take us out on to the Baseball Ground pitch and hit the crossbar from the 18-yard line, just to show us that he could do it, that he could play.

"He was young looking for his age, and amazingly fit, even though he'd contracted malaria when serving in the First World War. He always trained with us, advising, suggesting, correcting, and always in a quiet voice that still commanded our attention. Players felt immediately at ease in his presence. We got the impression that here was man who never made a promise unless he knew that he could fulfill it. His sincerity was complete and inspiring, and every member of the staff had the utmost confidence in him."

Ten days after Britain had celebrated VJ Day, Ted Magner set out on a new season with Derby County.

Goals Galore

ON 25 August 1945, the opening day of the transitional football season that would eventually take the game from its wartime footing back to a normal peacetime format, Derby County beat Fulham 5-2. There were no "first" and "second' championships, no matches counting double for both the league and the cup. There were simply 22 clubs, playing each other twice to give each a programme of 42 matches, just like before the war. The only difference was regionalisation, with the pre-war First and Second Division clubs split into the Football League North and Football League South. Along with Nottingham Forest, the Rams were the northernmost of the clubs in the southern division. Teams were still allowed to field up to six guest players.

One Derby County player involved in another aspect of the new format was Sammy Crooks, who was now chairman of the Players' Union. The Football League ruled that players who were now full-time – in other words they had been demobbed from the armed forces – would be paid £8 per week. But players still in the services – and therefore drawing pay from the Government – would be paid £4 per match. Crooks argued that it was wholly unfair that players like Stanley Matthews, Tommy Lawton, and, indeed, Raich Carter, would be paid only half the amount that some of their teammates would receive. "We want equality for all," said Crooks. Actually, when they were called upon to play three games in a week, the service players suddenly found themselves much better off than their full-time teammates, and that wasn't taking into account army pay and so on. Eventually, the League scrapped the service match fee.

A crowd of 15,000 saw the opening match of 1945-46 at the Baseball Ground. Two of the Rams' goals came from the 32-year-old Tottenham Hotspur centre-forward, Colin Lyman. Yet the *Derby Evening Telegraph* reporter was not overly impressed: "I am loath to criticise any player on his performance in the first game of the season, but let me make one suggestion It is addressed to Lyman, and is simply this: as a centre-forward try to be less of an individual and more of a leader."

Lyman would play only three more times before returning to Spurs, although the same writer did concede that both his goals against Fulham – which came in the first half together with one from Dally Duncan – were "spectacular". Angus Morrison and Tommy Powell scored in the second half, with Fulham's craggy-faced Ronnie Rooke netting either side of the interval. Fulham supporter (and soon to be a director) Tommy Trinder, "the Funny Comedian", watched the game from the Baseball Ground directors' box but must have found very little about which to laugh.

Neither Carter nor Doherty was available for the Rams that day. In fact Carter was scoring twice for Sunderland in a 6-3 defeat at Hillsborough, and he would be a regular member of the Wearsiders' line-up for the first four months of the season. It would be early December before he made his first appearance for the Rams, shortly after which he was transferred to Derby. Doherty was back the following week, however, as the Rams lost 2-1 to Fulham – the fixtures for 1945-46 saw clubs play each other home and away on consecutive weeks – and he scored the Rams' goal in the return game at Craven Cottage.

The following Saturday, Plymouth Argyle were hammered 4-0 at the Baseball Ground, Newport County were twice beaten 4-1 in October, and West Ham shipped five goals at Derby and three at Upton Park in the space of eight November days. Angus Morrison was finding the net regularly. At White Hart Lane on Christmas Day, Morrison scored twice in the Rams' 5-2 win. Thirty-three thousand fans had seen Spurs take a 2-1 half-time lead but Derby were too good for them. But for the fine form of Spurs' goalkeeper Jack Hall, the Londoners might have conceded another five on Boxing Day. As it was, the Rams had to settle for a 2-0 win.

In mid-January, Millwall lost 8-1 at Derby – Morrison scored his second hat-trick of the season – and the same player scored another three when Southampton were beaten 8-1 at the Baseball Ground in February. Jack Stamps also scored a hat-trick that day. The pre-war forward was available regularly again after being demobbed from the Royal Artillery. By now, the FA Cup campaign had begun, the first since Portsmouth had won it in 1939. Pompey had thus held on to the trophy for seven years. The Rams were about to take it from them, and Jack Stamps would have a huge say in the matter.

Slaughtered by the Rams

ON 5 January 1946, Derby County travelled to Kenilworth Road for the first leg of their third-round FA Cup-tie against Luton Town. For the first time in the competition's history, up to the quarter-finals the ties would be played on a home-and-away basis. On the face of it, Luton provided no great threat to the Rams. The Hatters, who had finished 1938-39 in the middle of the Second Division, were struggling along in the interim Football League South against the likes of Arsenal and Chelsea. They still had to meet Derby County in the league but the Rams were scoring goals, lots of goals, and fielded one of the best forward lines in the country with wartime guests Raich Carter and Peter Doherty both now signed permanently, centre-forward Jack Stamps, pre-war England winger Sammy Crooks, and Angus

Morrison, who could play at centre-forward but on this day was switched to the left wing in place of the injured Dally Duncan.

So Luton supporters probably feared the worst, but that did not dissuade them. Queues began forming long before the Kenilworth Road gates were opened, and, according to the *Derby Evening Telegraph*, "Luton supporters gave the Rams a terrific welcome as Jack Nicholas led them on to the field".

After ten minutes, Crooks put Derby in front with a lob into the right-hand corner of George Duke's net. Ten minutes after that, Stamps headed in the Rams' second goal, and before half-time Doherty had made it 3-0 (*modern statistical books show Carter as the scorer but contemporary newspaper reports all credit Doherty*). After the interval the traffic was similarly one-way as Stamps completed a second-half hat-trick to give him four in the match, and Derby a 6-0 lead in the tie, leaving one Hatters fan spluttering to the *Evening Telegraph* reporter: "What a combination! We'll be slaughtered at the Baseball Ground."

The reporter told readers: "Five minutes after the start, the result was inevitable. Luton were never in the same class as Derby County, who played exactly as they chose – surprisingly fast in the mud – and for most of the game had the Luton players running round in circles.

"Individualism – an ominous word when related to football – was completely absent. Each goal was the result of clever, unselfish teamwork, with the forward in the best position finishing off the concerted movement of brilliant scheming and complete understanding.

"Doherty was the architect of victory. He was hardworking, inspiring, dazzling. Several times when in front of the goal, he passed to a colleague who was in a better position.

"I do not want to detract from Stamps's grand performance – he was always in the right place at the right time – but he scored his four goals because he took the perfect openings that were made for him.

"Morrison bewildered with his speed … Carter sent in several terrific shots, but for the most part he played a delightfully constructive game. His close passes and tricks repeatedly spreadeagled the defence … Engineered by Doherty, executed by Carter, and finished off by Stamps – that was the formula for most of Derby's goals.

"Sammy Crooks outwitted all attempts to stop him … His goal had the touch of genius. He was well placed to shoot hard, but seeing the goalkeeper advancing towards him, Crooks lifted it over Duke's head into the net. Many other players would have slammed it and probably missed the net.

"… Leuty's clearance off the goal-line, when Needham slashed the ball across the goalmouth to the far corner, was a miracle. Apart from the groans of disappointment, even the Luton supporters applauded him."

On the following Wednesday afternoon supporters began arriving at the Baseball Ground well before the 2pm kick-off. The sight of military police and their RAF counterparts checking servicemen as they entered the ground greeted the fans. Despite the inevitability of the tie's result, there was still massive interest, not just to see the Rams but also simply to see an FA Cup game. The last one played at the Baseball Ground had been back in January 1939, when Everton had won 1-0 in the third round. Tim Ward could not play in the second leg against Luton. He was still serving the army and his leave was over. As the Rams ran out on a chill, damp and overcast Wednesday afternoon, Ward was travelling back to barracks, this time not to the horrors of war, however, but to the British Army of the Rhine (BAOR) football team that would one day be dubbed "Football's Vera Lynns" for their work in entertaining troops, not with a song but with a ball. Into Ward's place at left-half stepped Tommy Eggleston, who had been on the Rams' books since 1936 without ever playing a first-team game in peacetime. Like Ward, this would be his only FA Cup appearance of 1945-46.

Derby, playing in unfamiliar black and white striped shirts – in the event of a colour clash in the FA Cup, both teams had to change – were soon on the attack as the Luton defence battled into a howling wind. That wind, the muddy pitch, and the fact that the tie was now a foregone conclusion, provided a combination far from conducive to an entertaining football match, and when the first goal arrived, midway through the first half, its messy execution summed up the game. Duke failed to hold the ball and Carter, falling, managed to poke it into the net.

The Rams' second goal, five minutes later, was a pretty effort, however. Doherty dribbled through the Luton defence before slipping a perfect pass to Carter who slid the ball home, watching in satisfaction, with his hands on his hips, as it rolled over the line and nestled in the back of Duke's net. At the other end, Goodyear got the ball in the Rams' net "but the referee disregarded all claims for a goal on the score of offside". Thereafter, the game bobbled back and forth, without further incident worthy of report it seems, until, with literally the very last kick of the match, Morrison made it 3-0 on the day and 9-0 on aggregate.

The *Derby Evening Telegraph* reporter hadn't particularly enjoyed it: "Both wingers were undistinguished and Stamps had one of those exasperating days when the ball did not run kindly for him … Once again the Derby defence down the middle was not flawless but the Luton forwards were unable to turn their chances to good account."

Now all ears turned to the wireless, to see who next stood in Derby County's way.

Saturday, 5 January 1946, Third round, first leg
Luton Town 0
Derby County 6 *Stamps 4, Crooks, Doherty*
Luton Town: Duke; Beach, Dunsmore; Goodyear, Vinall, Campbell; Daniel, Brice, D.Needham, Gardiner, Waugh.
Derby County: Boulton; Nicholas, Parr; Bullions, Leuty, Ward; Crooks, Carter, Stamps, Doherty, Morrison
Referee: W. F. Daley (Ilford)
Attendance: 16,792

Wednesday, 9 January 1946, Third round, second leg
Derby County 3 *Carter (2), Morrison*
Luton Town 0
(Derby won 9-0 on aggregate)
Derby County: Boulton; Nicholas, Parr; Bullions, Leuty, Eggleston; Crooks, Carter, Stamps, Doherty, Morrison
Luton Town: Duke; Lake, Dunsmore; Goodyear, Gager, Campbell; Isaacs, Daniel, D.Needham, Vinall, Waugh.
Referee: W. F. Daley (Ilford)
Attendance: 16,629

Such Supreme Confidence

AFTER years of moderate attendances in the upside-down world of wartime football, with its remarkable scores and bizarre line-ups, there was enormous interest among the nation's football fans in 1945-46. The return of an almost-normal Football League competition, and, more significantly, of the FA Cup, had brought supporters flooding back through the turnstiles. Derby County fans were no exception and 20,000 attendances were becoming commonplace for League South matches at the Baseball Ground.

On Saturday, 26 January 1946, the Rams enjoyed their biggest crowd since the visit of Everton on Boxing Day 1938. Almost 32,000 crammed into a ground where the capacity had been reduced because of bomb damage caused during the heavy air-raid of 15 January 1941, when several people had lost their lives, many more were injured, and 1,650 house were damaged, many of them near the LMS Station, on which a dozen bombs had fallen, and the Baseball Ground whose double-decker Osmaston Stand had been hit. The gaunt ruins of the stand were a reminder of less happy times but the desire to see the game was so great that "numbers of spectators clambered on the dangerous stand" that would normally have housed 6,000, while Ley's foundry workers perched precariously on the roof of the Popular Side.

They all wanted to see the fourth-round FA Cup-tie first-leg game against West Bromwich Albion, and checkers dealing with the crowds swarming around outside were warned to watch out for counterfeit tickets believed to have been circulated at black-market prices after all the genuine tickets had been snapped up. During the morning hundreds of West Brom supporters without tickets had arrived in Derby and many had paid double and even treble for the forgeries being sold in streets leading to the ground.

Holders of genuine tickets were taking no chances. In order to be in good time, thousands of fans ate packed lunches in the streets and in public houses, and three hours before the 2.30pm kick-off, queues had formed at the turnstiles. Groups of ticket hunters gathered in Shaftesbury Crescent, waiting to make a dash to bid high prices for tickets when individuals offered them.

When the gates were opened at 1pm, several thousand fans streamed through the turnstiles and on to the terraces, anxious to obtain the best vantage points. An hour later it was estimated that there were 20,000 people in the ground, and by kick-off the number had swelled to an official figure of 31,795. That does not include those who settled for paying Ley's one shilling to stand on the roof of one of the firm's workshops. The view was restricted, to say the least, but the money went to a good cause, the Red Cross.

The boys' enclosure was soon spilling over, and some youngsters were allowed to sit behind the Normanton goal. Even then, about 100 boys wandered around the narrow cinder track, looking for a place on the tightly packed terraces. As the teams emerged, a number of adults followed the boys' example and also swarmed on to the touchline in the hope of finding a less uncomfortable spot elsewhere. Police and club officials were kept busy diplomatically shepherding the wandering fans back into the crowd. Wherever they ended up they were to be rewarded by a game packed with thrills from the first minute to the last after the Rams took to the field under a new manager.

His "agreement" with Derby County at an end, Ted Magner had left to take up an appointment with FC Metz, the French club that he had coached before the war. Magner's heart, it seemed, was always on the Continent. His replacement as Derby County manager was a pub landlord. Stuart McMillan had played one League match for the Rams at the start of a long career that also saw him serve several other clubs including Wolves, Chelsea and Bradford City. He had also played four games of first-class cricket for Derbyshire, and his father, Johnny McMillan, had scored 50 goals for the Rams in the 1890s. Stuart McMillan was running the Nag's Head at Mickleover when he inherited a football team good enough to win the FA Cup.

With Dally Duncan now fit to take his place on the left wing, Morrison moved back to centre-forward, with Stamps making way. Luck was not with the Rams. In the first minute, after what turned out to be one of the finest movements in the game, they should have taken the lead. Some brilliant inter-passing between Peter Doherty, Raich Carter and Reg Harrison (who had replaced the injured Crooks) saw Morrison in a position to head Derby in front, but Doherty inadvertently deflected the ball away from the centre-forward with his head.

Later, Doherty headed against the crossbar with the brilliant goalkeeper Jim Sanders – who, in the 1960s, was to become landlord of the Albert Vaults in Derby – well beaten. And in the last minute, all the Derby players were convinced that they should have been awarded a penalty after Sanders appeared to pull Doherty down.

It was Doherty who scored the only goal of the game, spot on the hour-mark. He netted after good work by the former Derby Corinthian, Harrison, who had not arrived back home in Derby until 4.30am that day, after travelling through the night from his army camp.

Four days later, the sides met again at The Hawthorns, where almost 38,000 found time off on a Wednesday afternoon to witness the second leg. Among them was the mayor of Derby, Alderman Thomas Johnson

This time, the Rams got their just desserts, despite being "blinded at times by a raging storm of hail and snow". Carter gave them the lead in the 25th minute, coolly lifting the ball over Sanders's head and into the far corner of the net after Harrison's cross,

Derby held their lead until the 52nd minute, when, against the run of play, Albion equalised through Ike Clarke, following one of the best moves in the match.

Eight minutes later, however, Harrison's centre was handled in the area and up stepped Jack Stamps, playing at inside-left in place of the injured Doherty, to restore the Rams' lead from the penalty-spot. In the 79th minute, Harrison completed the scoring after Duncan had swung the ball across. Derby 4-1 on aggregate.

It had been a difficult game for both teams with that snow and hail being interspersed with rain, sunshine and a gusting wind. The *Derby Evening Telegraph* reporter: "As a team the Rams have rarely played better, and the defence certainly touched the peak of its form. Parr played like an international at times ... the dominant Leuty played even better than he did at Derby on Saturday. The centre-half was in one of his most aggressive moods, and it was reassuring to see him tackle so quickly and with such supreme confidence. Nicholas, as usual, gave his two colleagues admirable support.

"Bullions and Musson fell into the scheme of things with so much success ... but I daresay that they will be the first to admit that they received considerable help from Stamps and Carter, who proved a great 'general' in the absence of Doherty. Though not so spectacular as Carter, Stamps fitted in exceptionally well ... Carter acted as the link between halves and forwards, and it was his uncanny ball distribution and his readiness to try shots that seemed to upset the Albion defence " ... While Morrison failed to get a goal, the young Scot simply refused to stay put and if he was not out on the wings he could be seen in the middle harassing the Albion defenders into making hasty clearances. Harrison was concerned in all three goals. Duncan was more impressive in midfield ..."

Hitherto, supporters had been grateful just to have the FA Cup back. Now they were just beginning to wonder if the Rams could go all the way.

Saturday, 26 January 1946, Fourth round, first leg
Derby County 1 *Doherty*
West Bromwich Albion 0
Derby County: Boulton; Nicholas, Parr; Bullions, Leuty, Musson; Harrison, Carter, Morrison, Doherty, Duncan
West Bromwich Albion: Sanders; C.Shaw, Kinsell; Witcomb, Tranter, Millard; Elliott, Clarke, Newsome, Connelly, Butler.
Referee: P. Snape (Manchester)
Attendance: 31,795

Wednesday, 30 January 1946, Fourth round, second leg
West Bromwich Albion 1 *Clarke*
Derby County 3 *Carter, Stamps (pen), Harrison*
(Derby won 4-1 on aggregate)
West Bromwich Albion: Sanders; C.Shaw, Kinsell; Witcomb, Tranter, Millard; Elliott, Clarke, Newsome, Connelly, Butler.
Derby County: Boulton; Nicholas, Parr; Bullions, Leuty, Musson; Harrison, Carter, Morrison, Stamps, Duncan
Referee: P. Snape (Manchester)
Attendance: 37,734

Brighton Rocked

BY February 1946, the odds on Derby County winning the first post-war FA Cup had shortened to 5/1. In the fifth round they faced Brighton and Hove Albion, of the curiously named transitional Third Division South (South), with Brighton enjoying home advantage in the first leg. When the Rams came away from the Goldstone Ground with a 4-1 first-leg advantage, the bookies shaved another couple of points off that price.

Less than 20 Rams fans made the long journey to the South Coast, and they saw two goals each from Peter Doherty and Raich Carter put Derby through, but it was not as easy as it appeared. The *Derby Evening Telegraph* told readers: "Derby County's one mistake was a tendency, twice displayed, to believe that class alone would tell. The first time was in the opening minute, when Doherty started as though he would give an exhibition of how to play football. The second occasion was just after they scored their first goal in the opening half, Derby again resorting to 'classic' methods.

"Albion wouldn't have it. They kicked, they rushed, they tackled – robustly and cleanly – and all they lacked was a little good fortune in finishing. If their plan of campaign in that opening minute had been attended by any luck, we might have had a Cup shock, or at least an early goal from Brighton."

In difficult conditions – the game was played throughout in a fierce wind – Doherty gave Derby the lead in the 33rd minute. Carter netted the second seven minutes after the interval, and Stan Willemse, later to win a League championship medal with Chelsea, scored Brighton's only goal after 60 minutes. Nine minutes from time, Carter got the Rams' third; four minutes later, Doherty completed the scoring from the penalty spot.

Despite their plucky display, Brighton were thus compelled to travel to Derby for the second leg with no hope of anything more encouraging than to discover by how many goals they would ultimately lose.

Yet even though the Rams' passage into the quarter-finals was now a foregone conclusion, and despite the Wednesday afternoon kick-off, there were still 32,000 at the Baseball Ground. This time, however, the ticket touts had a bad day. It appeared that hardly anyone had gone to the ground that afternoon unless they already had a ticket. The result was that, instead of selling the tickets on which they had speculated, at a large profit, the touts were forced to offload them at face value, or even at a loss. Fans queuing at the turnstiles jeered the would-be racketeers.

Those who had already paid to get in were rewarded with a goal glut from the Rams. Derby's supremacy was obvious from the start, and after nine minutes they had extended their overall lead to five goals. First Doherty put the Rams ahead, banging the ball into an empty net after the Brighton goalkeeper, Harry Baldwin, had failed to hold a shot from Morrison. Then Carter made it 2-0 on the day, lobbing the ball over Baldwin's head after the goalkeeper changed his mind about coming out and began to retreat towards his line.

Four minutes later, Carter scored again when Baldwin knocked the forward's header against the crossbar and then had to watch as it dropped over the line. Six minutes before half-time, Doherty had added his second. Carter's hat-trick goal came in the 52nd minute; two minutes later, veteran winger Sammy Crooks made it 6-0 on the afternoon, and 10-1 on aggregate.

The Rams' early successes had come courtesy of some defensive errors, Carter's first two goals alone being laid on a plate by the Brighton goalkeeper. Yet the *Evening Telegraph* reporter did not think that this affected the overall result: "Well as Wilson, Whent and Willemse played, the Brighton defenders were unable to find an answer to the tricks of Carter and Doherty; the thrustful Morrison, the crafty Crooks, who beat Watson at will; and, on occasion, the brilliant Duncan. The Rams could have had more goals – particularly the two inside wizards, Carter and Doherty – but on more than one occasion they refused to rub it in.

"Morrison also missed chances, but I give him full marks for taking Risdon away from the middle and thereby leaving a clear path for Doherty. For the most part, the home men played with restraint, and not a little embroidery, but had it been a more serious match, I should have been alarmed to see the Brighton forwards get so much of the ball.

"Leuty was sound enough, and there was little wrong with the two backs, Nicholas and Parr, but the two wing-halves, Bullions and Musson, were not impressive, despite the fact that Doherty and Carter repeatedly went back to do the fetching. The Brighton forwards fought back spiritedly, but they lacked a schemer and a marksman."

The Rams were through, though, and faced much tougher opposition – Aston Villa. Two epic struggles were now in prospect as Derby County moved nearer their Wembley destiny.

Saturday, 9 February 1946, Fifth round, first leg
Brighton & Hove Albion 1 *Willemse*
Derby County 4 *Doherty (2; 1 pen), Carter (2)*
Brighton & Hove Albion: Baldwin; Marriott, Watson; Wilson, Risdon, J. Whent; Longdon, Moore, Davie, S.Willemse, Stephens
Derby County: Boulton; Nicholas, Parr; Bullions, Leuty, Musson; Harrison, Carter, Morrison, Doherty, Duncan
Referee: Lieutenant Commander G .J. Clarke (London)
Attendance: 22,000

Wednesday, 13 February 1946, Fifth round, second leg

Derby County 6 *Carter (3), Doherty (2), Crooks*
Brighton & Hove Albion 0

Derby won 10-1 on aggregate

Derby County: Boulton; Nicholas, Parr; Bullions, Leuty, Musson; Crooks, Carter, Morrison, Doherty, Duncan

Brighton & Hove Albion: Baldwin; Marriott, Watson; Wilson, Risdon, J. Whent; Hindley, Moore, Davie, S.Willemse, Stephens

Referee: Lieutenant Commander G. J. Clarke (London)
Attendance: 32,000

A Test of
Endurance

D ERBY County supporters would have done almost
anything to gain admission to their club's FA Cup
ties in 1946. The first post-war competition was
drawing bumper crowds, and on 2 March, at Villa Park for
the first leg of the quarter-final between the Rams and Aston
Villa, the attendance was 76,588, still a ground record today.
A relief train reinforced five service trains from Derby LMS
station and together they carried 1,200 people to the match
that Saturday morning.

However, some fans had travelled from Derby on the
Friday evening and they walked the streets of Birmingham
in freezing temperatures in the small hours. By 9.30am all
roads leading to Villa's grand old stadium "were thronged
with crowds and Rams supporters wearing black and white

favours were prominent among the early arrivals". In fact, so many people had allowed themselves plenty of time that, with 45 minutes still to go to kick-off, tramcars were running empty to Villa Park. Everyone was already there, some of the Rams fans sporting wartime steel helmets painted black and white.

Although before setting off for Birmingham many supporters had taken the trouble to vote in the first Derbyshire County Council elections to be held since 1937, many more had taken what the *Evening Telegraph* described as "French leave". Ley's had given workers permission to be absent on Saturday morning, but a machine moulder at an Ilkeston foundry was suspended for taking time off to watch the match. Sixty of his colleagues came out on strike. Elsewhere, Mr F. Gudgeon, works manager of International Combustion, said that "a good number" of workers had absented themselves and that production had been affected. "They obviously think that football is more important than getting the work done," he said. Qualcast reported that absenteeism had been light but that production had still been affected.

The match was a real rollercoaster affair, and a real test for goalkeeper Bill Townsend. Townsend was making his peacetime debut for the Rams, who now had a major goalkeeping worry. Three days after demolishing Brighton in the second-leg, Derby had beaten Swansea Town 2-1 at the Baseball Ground in a bad-tempered Football League South match. But the victory had come at a cost. Swansea's tough centre-forward, Trevor Ford, had clattered Frank Boulton so heavily that twice the goalkeeper had to leave the field. On both occasions Jack Nicholas took over in goal and the Rams played on with ten men. Boulton's injury was so severe that he was later admitted to Derbyshire Royal Infirmary and at one stage it was feared that he had suffered internal injuries. Happily, he was to recover, but he would be out of action for at least a month. At first Don Bilton, signed from Wolves at the start of the 1944-45 season, was drafted in before Townsend replaced him for the Villa cup-tie.

Stuart McMillan had tried to sign a longer-term replacement when he asked Leicester City about Alick Grant but Leicester wanted £5,000. Grant would join the Rams the following season for £1,000, a similar fee to that which Derby now paid for Boulton's replacement who, though, was not signed in time to play in the quarter-final. Former England goalkeeper Vic Woodley had last played against the Rams that September, when he'd saved a Jack Nicholas penalty for Chelsea at Stamford Bridge. By the time the Rams came calling for his services, Woodley was in semi-retirement with Bath City in the Southern League, although Derby still had to deal with Chelsea over his transfer. Woodley would be available for the FA Cup semi-final – if the Rams got past Villa.

So it was Townsend who was in goal at Villa Park, and after only six minutes he was picking the ball out of his net after George Edwards put the home team ahead. But Doherty equalised in the 23rd, lashing Carter's headed pass home via a post. Five minutes later, Jack Iverson gave Villa a half-time lead, but in the 62nd minute Carter equalised again following Dally Duncan's cross.

The scores were level for only four minutes before Frank Broome – later to star for Derby – made it 3-2; surely the

Rams could not equalise a third time? But, with five minutes to play, Doherty scored his second with a header from Duncan's low cross … and still the game was not over.

The finale belonged to Sammy Crooks. With only 60 seconds to play, he latched on to a loose ball and crashed it goalwards. As the ball bulged the net, Crooks ran back towards the halfway line, clapping his hands above his head. But even this legendary winger's sprinting prowess did not prevent him from being swamped by ecstatic colleagues.

It was, said the *Derby Evening Telegraph*, "a thrill-packed game with enough goals to satisfy the most goal-hungry fan".

Derby County received 100,000 applications for second-leg tickets, and their scheme for selling these at a reserve match disgusted some fans, who wrote letters to the *Evening Telegraph*, signing themselves "Fair Play" and "Cup-Tied". Come match day itself, some that could afford it were prepared to pay £4 for a 3s (15p) ticket on the black market.

The first person to arrive on that following Saturday was 14-year-old Clifford Jones of Birkinstyle Lane, Shirland. He walked up to a Baseball Ground turnstile at spot-on 10am and waited for two and a half hours until it opened, by which time the queue behind him stretched for a quarter of a mile. "I wanted to make sure that I didn't miss it," he told a reporter. In the end, 32,000 wedged themselves into the bomb-damaged Baseball Ground. They were rewarded with another dramatic game.

After 30 minutes, Rams fans were in a state of panic. Crooks had been carried off with a leg injury after a clattering from "Mush" Callaghan, the tough Villa wing-half who had been decorated for gallantry after saving the lives of three people during an air-raid on Birmingham four years earlier. And Villa's former England forward, Frank Broome, had levelled the aggregate after a fumble by Townsend, whose appearance in goal for the first-leg had been his first match for the Rams at any level for two years.

It was Raich Carter who changed it all. Just before half-time, Duncan took a free-kick and Carter headed his 13th goal in 12 games. Then Villa lost Harry Parkes with a dislocated elbow. The 1-1 draw put Derby into the semi-final. Peter Doherty felt that, in the end, the tie "had virtually resolved itself into a test of endurance".

Referring to his dramatic late winner in the first leg, the *Evening Telegraph* told readers: "It must be a pleasant, if piquant, thought for Sammy Crooks, as he nurses his leg injury tonight, that at least he was in the Derby County v Aston Villa sixth-round Cup-tie long enough to decide the issue."

The *Telegraph* reporter summed up the second leg: "Derby in effect decided to carry on without a right winger, and it is greatly to Duncan's credit that he responded so unsparingly to the extra calls made upon him … Stamps did not take advantage of his chances as a centre-forward should, but then Stamps makes no claim to be a centre-forward."

That last comment seems remarkable today, since Rams fans almost always think of Jack Stamps as a battering-ram centre-forward. In fact, he moved to leading the attack only late in the FA Cup-winning campaign. As that great player, Raich Carter, once told the author: "Make no mistake, Jackie Stamps was a fine footballing inside-forward."

The *Telegraph* continued: "Although Doherty practically played himself to a standstill, I regard Carter as the most valuable of the home forwards … acting as a one-man support of the front-line troops … by his shrewdly placed upfield passes.

"Having had occasion to criticise Musson with melancholy frequency it is with particular pleasure that I raise a hearty British cheer for his display in this match. He was never outpaced, his tackling was effective. Behind him, Jack Parr played one of his best games of the season … Leuty and Nicholas were also markedly successful … A rare stalwart, Nick!"

Footnote: On the same day that the Rams completed their sixth-round tie against Aston Villa, there was a tragedy at Burnden Park where 33 people were killed and over 500 more injured during the sixth-round tie between Bolton Wanderers and Stoke City. The game was held up for 25 minutes and then, remarkably so it seems today, resumed and played to its conclusion.

Saturday, 2 March 1946, Sixth round, first leg

Aston Villa 3 *Edwards, Iverson, Broome*
Derby County 4 *Doherty (2) Carter, Crooks*
Aston Villa: Wakeman, Potts, Cummings: F.Moss, Parkes, E.Lowe; Goffin, Broome, Edwards, Iverson, Smith.
Derby County: Townsend; Nicholas, Parr; Bullions, Leuty, Musson; Crooks, Carter, Stamps, Doherty, Duncan
Referee: W. E. Ross-Gower (London)
Attendance: 76,588

Saturday, 9 March 1946, Sixth round, second leg

Derby County 1 *Carter*
Aston Villa 1 *Broome*

Derby won 5-4 on aggregate

Derby County: Townsend; Nicholas, Parr; Bullions, Leuty, Musson; Crooks, Carter, Stamps, Doherty, Duncan

Aston Villa: Wakeman, Potts, Cummings: Parkes, Callaghan, E.Lowe; Goffin, Broome, Edwards, Iverson, Smith.

Referee: W. E. Ross-Gower (London)
Attendance: 32,000

(Left) Peter Doherty pictured with the Midland Cup in 1945. He scored five in the Baseball Ground leg of the Final against Aston Villa.

(Bottom, left) Ted Magner, the highly regarded coach who put together the Rams FA Cup-winning team.

(Bottom, right) Stuart McMillan, a former Rams player and Derbyshire cricketer, was landlord of the Nag's Head at Mickleover when the Rams board asked him to take over as manager.

Peter Doherty (diving, extreme left) heads the Rams' third goal at Villa Park to draw his side level in the first leg of the FA Cup quarter-final.

Jack Parr and Vic Woodley can do nothing to prevent Ambrose Mulraney from scoring in the drawn FA Cup semi-final match at Hillsborough.

The Rams line-up for the first semi-final at Hillsborough: back row (left to right): Reg Harrison, Jack Parr, Vic Woodley, Jim Bullions, Leon Leuty, Jack Stamps. Front tow: Chick Musson, Raich Carter, Jack Nicholas, Peter Doherty, Dally Duncan.

Programme for the first semi-final.

Cartoonist's view of the Hillsborough semi-final.

A Noise Like Thunder

At two o'clock in the morning of Wednesday, 20 March 1946, the Derby County office staff of five, who had been working all night to prepare tickets for the Rams' FA Cup semi-final against Birmingham City at Hillsborough in three days' time, were just about to go home when someone pointed out that hundreds of supporters had been camped outside since 11pm. With stools, sandwiches and even coke braziers, the fans were clearly prepared to wait through the night until the ticket office opened at 9am. Some residents of Shaftesbury Crescent came out with cups of tea and coffee. Eventually, the Rams decided to open the ticket office in the small hours. The staff that were about to go home took off their coats and set to work again. Each club had an allotment of 21,500 tickets, most of them at 2s 6d (13p)

each for the Hillsborough terracing. Nobody was allowed to purchase more than one ticket, but many hardy souls simply went to the back of the long queue, which stretched into Hartington Street, and started again. Throughout that Wednesday morning supporters shuffled slowly forward. There were plenty of women and children in the queue. Many wives had joined it in order to buy tickets for their husbands who had to go to work. One woman wanted eight tickets. She was told that she could have only one. That she had queued for three and a half hours made no difference.

Three days later, by road and rail, thousands of people left Derby for Sheffield – "the biggest exodus the town has seen since the pre-war holiday periods" claimed the *Derby Evening Telegraph*. A similar number made the journey from Birmingham. Their trains came though Derby, meaning that relief trains again had to be organised because normal services would already be packed by the time they reached the East Midlands. As one train carrying Rams fans built up a head of steam ready for the short journey north, a military train bound for a southern port was waiting on the opposite platform.

"Good old Derby! Put it across 'em!" shouted a soldier.

"Come and see us at Wembley!" came the answer.

As one relief train was loading with Derby supporters, a train laden with Birmingham fans clanked through the station. The Birmingham supporters hung out of the windows, sounding rattles and bells. "This is where you get off!" one Rams fan roared at them. A huge cheer went up.

It was about as much as either set of fans had to cheer about that day. In what was described as "a second-rate cup-tie" the teams played out a tame 1-1 semi-final draw. The Rams took the lead in only the fourth minute when Carter might have been pulled up for hands but was allowed to carry on and toe-poke the ball into an empty net as Birmingham's defenders waited in vain for the referee to blow his whistle and award them a free-kick. Ambrose Mulraney's 52nd-minute equaliser was a better affair, but around the goals there was much to forget.

Yet the Rams might have won it against a nervous Birmingham side managed by the former Derby and England forward, Harry Storer. Both Doherty and Carter had shots cleared off the line, and Doherty headed against the crossbar. But, according to "Mark Eaton" in the *Derby Evening Telegraph*, the Rams were simply "the better of two poor sides".

Sixty-five thousand fans had watched the Hillsborough game. It was a huge attendance, but it would be eclipsed by the replay, four days later. When young wing-half Jim Bullions sat nervously in the Maine Road dressing room, minutes before the semi-final replay was due to get under way, he thought he could hear thunder. The noise started as a low rumble, and slowly built up into a crescendo.

"We looked at each other, and wondered what on earth it was," Bullions recalled. "Then we realised that it was the noise of people's feet stamping on the wooden floor of the stand above us. I'd never heard anything like it. And when we ran out a few minutes later, I'd never seen anything like it, either."

As the Rams players emerged from the tunnel on that Wednesday afternoon, they realised that Maine Road was bursting at the seams. Terraces and stands were full to overflowing, with spectators wedged right up to the touchline. What the players could not have known was that they were about to become a part of football history. The crowd of 80,407 is still a record for a midweek game between two English clubs outside Wembley, and is unlikely ever to be beaten. Said Jim Bullions: "When we took throw-ins and corners, we had to move people out of the way. It was absolutely incredible."

The Rams were without centre-half Leon Leuty, who had injured a leg at Hillsborough. Into his place came Jack Howe for his first appearance in the FA Cup since 1939. When the Rams' current run had started, Howe had still been abroad in the army. Now he was 90 minutes from Wembley. Together with two Birmingham players, goalkeeper Gil Merrick and midfielder Fred Harris, Reg Harrison had been released from an army football trip to Luxembourg in order to play at Maine Road.

After 90 minutes there was still no score, but in the fifth minute of extra time, Peter Doherty reached Dally Duncan's cross a split second before Birmingham's Ted Duckhouse, to put the Rams ahead. The two players collided, and Duckhouse was carried off with a broken leg.

Raich Carter remembered: "I heard a crack and thought: 'Oh my God, Peter's broken his leg.' I didn't want either of them to be hurt, obviously, but I was so relieved when Peter stood up."

Poor Duckhouse was stretchered off, leaving Derby to run riot against ten men. Thirteen minutes into extra-time, Jack Stamps made it 2-0, sliding Duncan's pass beyond Merrick. Nine minutes later, Doherty dribbled up to Merrick before poking the ball between the goalkeeper's legs. And near the end, Stamps made it 4-0 from Raich Carter's pass, stabbing the ball into the roof of the net.

Yet it might have been different. In the 50th minute, Birmingham's Harold Bodle had only Vic Woodley to beat. But the former England goalkeeper kidded Bodle by leaving a huge gap – and Bodle was so surprised, he planted the ball straight into Woodley's midriff.

Whether the Rams would have equalised, no-one will ever know. The reality, however, was that Derby County were through to their first appearance in a Wembley FA Cup Final. They would meet Charlton Athletic who had beaten Bolton Wanderers 2-0 at the first time of asking.

Saturday, 23 March 1946, Semi-final (at Hillsborough, Sheffield)
Derby County 1 *Carter*
Birmingham City 1 *Mulraney*
Derby County: Woodley; Nicholas, Parr; Bullions, Leuty, Musson; Harrison, Carter, Stamps, Doherty, Duncan
Birmingham City: Merrick; Duckhouse, Jennings; Harris, Turner, Mitchell; Mulraney, Dougal, Jones, Bodle, Edwards.
Referee: W. H. E. Evans (Liverpool)
Attendance: 65,000

Wednesday, 27 March 1946, Semi-final replay (at Maine Road, Manchester)
Derby County 4 *Doherty (2), Stamps (2)*
Birmingham City 0
Derby County: Woodley; Nicholas, Parr; Bullions, Leuty, Musson; Harrison, Carter, Stamps, Doherty, Duncan
Birmingham City: Merrick; Duckhouse, Jennings; Harris, Turner, Mitchell; Mulraney, Dougal, Jones, Bodle, Edwards.
Referee: W. H. E. Evans (Liverpool)
Attendance: 80,407

One Million Tickets Sought

FOUR days after Derby County won their place in the 1946 FA Cup Final it was reported that "more than 100,000" Rams supporters wanted to buy a ticket for Wembley. If even one-third of them had also wished to purchase a season ticket, then the Baseball Ground's capacity would be regularly tested in 1946-47. Picking up on this, "Regular Supporter" wrote to the *Derby Evening Telegraph* suggesting that this was "an opportune moment to invite applications for season tickets for next year, and to allot one or more Cup Final tickets in respect of all such applications received". Then any tickets remaining could be drawn for "from the mixed bag of applications from all and sundry". It would, said "Regular Supporter", "very effectively curb the activities of 'gate-crashers and black market merchants'".

Sure enough, demand for Wembley tickets, if not for Baseball Ground season tickets, grew and grew. Five days later, the *Evening Telegraph* announced: "One Million Tickets Sought From Derby." The Baseball Ground ticket office was apparently buried under an avalanche of a quarter of a million letters that were being opened by Derby County office staff aided by six sorters borrowed from the Post Office as well as by gatemen and even by the players themselves. As each club would receive only 12,000 tickets, there were going to be an awful lot of very disappointed people.

When it came to football, Ley's Malleable Castings Co Ltd continued to be particularly enlightened employers. The works convenor, Mr C. H. Hudson, wrote to the *Evening Telegraph* to express his colleagues' gratitude for the company making it possible "for those employees who wished to attend important League matches and Cup-ties to do so. Since Derby County have qualified for the Cup Final the directors have further displayed their generosity by offering to reimburse 300 of their employees whose names have been drawn for the Cup Final tickets and also by meeting the expenses of the travelling involved".

That didn't go down well with supporters who were not fortunate enough to work for Ley's. "Without a Ticket" wrote of his disgust that Ley's had been allocated 300 tickets. Mr Hudson was quick to point out that this was not the case. Ley's had simply offered to pay for those tickets individually obtained by its employees. There was still much general disgruntlement, however. A woman writing on behalf of "Four Very Disgusted Popular-siders" – herself, husband and two brothers – said that they had missed only game all season (that through illness) and had often had to set off at 10.15am from Wirksworth in order to make 3pm kick-offs at the Baseball Ground. Now, she said, they saw people "who had never seen the Rams before" obtaining Cup Final tickets ahead of them. When these people got to Wembley, she said, they would have to consult the programme before they could tell which team was Derby County. She added: "PS: For sale, one black and white hand-knitted beret."

"Never Again," "Disgusted Supporter", "Once Again Disappointed", "Twenty Years A Supporter," and "Rain Or Shine Supporter" all had similar tales to tell. One claimed that in a Derby pub he had been offered "five 3s 6d ticket for 15 shillings each". The same fan also claimed to have been shown a "chit" that entitled one man to claim three Cup Final tickets, while another supporter alleged that many lucky recipients "have not had to write and waste 5d each and wait in suspense for 15 days to see if they would get a ticket. They have been sure of their tickets since it was know that Derby County were in the Final".

One of the main bones of contention among supporters was that the Rams had apparently no way of differentiating between regular supporters and casual spectators. Derby County's chairman, Ben Robshaw, issued a statement: "The Board have read with concern, letters in the *Derby Evening Telegraph* regarding the sale and distribution of Cup Final tickets and people having tickets in their possession last week. The tickets from the Football Association were in the custody of this Club's bank until Monday, 15 April 1946, so these tickets that were shown were previously issued from bodies outside the Derby County Football Club." It was a valid point.

The Derbyshire Football Association, for instance, would have received a separate allocation, although this would have been a mere handful and not so many as to flood the market as some disenchanted Rams believed.

★ ★ ★ ★ ★

While the ticket issue raged on, another controversy was taking up space in the *Derby Evening Telegraph*'s letters pages. On Wednesday, 10 April, Derby Town Council's special purposes committee had voted to give Derby County a civic welcome on their return whatever the result at Wembley. On 30 April the team would be met by the mayor at the borough boundary at Alvaston and then process into town to the police station. If the Rams won the Cup, then the journey would be made by open-topped bus. Moreover, on 6 May, the council would host a dinner for 250 people – players, directors, MPs and county and civic dignitaries.

As one might perhaps imagine, in those austere times of shortages and food rationing, the idea of a civic junket for the local football club – even if they had won the FA Cup – did not go down well with many locals. Letters soon began to appear in the *Derby Evening Telegraph*. J. R. Kendall of Chellaston thought that while meeting the players at the borough boundary was an excellent idea, "when one reads that this is to be followed by a dinner to about 250 people when every day one reads of world food shortages, economy etc … to allocate ratepayers' money for a function of this kind is open to criticism … would it not be more in keeping with the principles of the Council … that the occasion be symbolised by small gifts to the more needy townsfolk such as old-age pensioners?"

Mr A. Watson, of Hardwick Street, pointed out that on the same day as the Council's announcement, the Prime Minister had told the nation that "a letter has been sent to every civic head urging them to avoid waste of any food". "Any comments?" Mr Watson asked.

"Two Volunteer Workers" said that they were "amazed that in these times of austerity and famine, Derby Corporation should dream of spending the ratepayers' money on entertaining themselves and their friends". They asked: "Why not appropriate this money for the benefit of our wounded and disabled soldiers who fought and gave their limbs so that Derby County footballers should be able to play?"

Meanwhile, the newspaper's "Candid Column" weighed in: "All honour to Derby County for reaching the Cup Final, but this great achievement does not warrant the squandering of precious food for 250 people. That part of the Corporation's welcome home to the players and officials of the club should be cancelled … in these crucial days of food scarcity, both at home and on the Continent, a dinner for 250 guests cannot be justified."

When plans for the dinner were mentioned at a meeting of the Derby Food Control Committee, Mr A. Houseman, the deputy food executive officer, said that it would probably be done through British Restaurants, the communal kitchens created in 1940 to help people who had been bombed out of their homes, had run out of food ration coupons, or who otherwise needed help. They were still operating in peacetime and would not be disbanded in 1947. Mr Houseman said that, in his opinion, no special authority would be needed for the meal. A member of the committee added: "If they win the Cup, we don't mind giving them a bit of a feed."

On 17 April, however, the Council bowed to public pressure. The mayor, Alderman Thomas Johnson, told the *Evening Telegraph* that it "in view of the food situation it was felt that a reception … along the lines of that given to American troops … would be more acceptable than a dinner". So, on the evening of 6 May, a reception, concert and dance would be held at Bemrose School.

The same day as the announcement, the *Evening Telegraph* reported that Cornish new potatoes were now available in Derby – at ten shillings per pound – and English asparagus was for sale at £1 5s 0d per bunch. The average weekly in Britain was just over £7. No wonder many people had been angered by plans for a civic meal for some footballers.

Injury Worries

WHILE many people were preoccupied with obtaining tickets and preventing civic dinners, the Rams still had a league programme to complete, and on the Wednesday evening of 3 April they suffered a major blow when right-back Jack Parr suffered a fractured right-arm during the Football League South match against Luton Town at the Baseball Ground. There were less than five minutes remaining when Parr fell heavily in a tackle, and although he carried on to the final whistle – the Rams won 4-3 – immediately after the match the defender was taken to the Derbyshire Royal Infirmary where an X-ray revealed a fractured radius bone.

It was not a complicated injury but one that normally took about six weeks to heal. Parr's Cup Final looked in serious doubt. For the player it was a particularly devastating blow. According to the *Derby Evening Telegraph*, "Parr had been playing like an international".

The Rams had other injury worries. Against Luton, Frank Boulton was back in goal because Woodley, who was now a part-time footballer and employed on essential work in a Slough factory, had caught his right hand in a machine and suffered cuts to two fingers. Sammy Crooks was still sidelined following his clattering against Aston Villa, and Dally Duncan and Leon Leuty had also missed the Luton game because of injuries. Duncan had dislocated a finger on his right hand after falling at Maine Road. Leuty was still suffering from the leg injury that had kept him of the replay.

When the Rams met Aston Villa in a league game on 6 April, none of the injured foursome had recovered and Boulton was also missing. The goalkeeper had been brought back too soon for the home game against Luton. His confidence had been badly affected by the clash with Trevor Ford. With Woodley still nursing cut fingers, and Boulton now continuing his rehabilitation against Everton Reserves, the Rams looked for their sixth goalkeeper of the season after those two, Townsend, Bilton and the Queen of the South player, Savage.

They found him in the shape of the eccentric Wynn Griffiths, a veterinary surgeon who had been working for the War Agricultural Committee at Weybridge and playing as an amateur in Arsenal's first team while on loan from Cardiff City. In his mid-20s, Griffiths had played for the Gunners against the touring Moscow Dynamo side in 1945 when he had to be replaced at half-time after being kicked on the head. At Villa Park he left in four goals but in the *Derby Evening Telegraph*, "Mark Eaton" commented: "It is a long time since I saw a more daring or spectacular display of goalkeeping, and though he made me shudder once or twice when he ran yards out of his charge, one must congratulate him on his remarkable anticipation or judgment … on one occasion he pounced on the ball in almost cat-like fashion. He certainly saved the Rams from a heavier defeat, even though he had luck on occasions."

However, Wynn Griffiths never again played for Derby County. Two days later an X-ray revealed that against Villa he had cracked a vertebra and was ruled out for the season. Griffiths did not disappear altogether, however. After the Football League resumed, he played once for Cardiff City, three times for Newport County, and later owned racehorses, claimed to have attended more consecutive Epsom Derbies – 60 – than anyone else alive, and until 2000 was employed as a racing tipster for BBC Radio Wales. He died in 2006, aged 86, almost 60 years to the day since he helped out the Rams.

With Woodley still not fit, and Boulton not considered confident enough, Derby County used their seventh goalkeeper of the season when Bill Allsop, a local player, played in the next two league matches, a 4-1 defeat of Leicester City at the Baseball Ground, and a 1-0 defeat by Aston Villa, also at Derby. Leuty and Duncan had both recovered to play in those two games. There was also hope of Crooks returning to the first team. He had made three appearances for the Reserves before a freak incident involving a punctured car tyre brought him right back into the reckoning. On the way back from watching the FA Amateur Cup Final at Middlesbrough, Crooks's car suffered its fifth puncture of the trip. The great Rams favourite took one look at the tyre and, in sheer frustration, kicked it. Miraculously his knee locked back into place and he was fit enough to play in the league match at Charlton, just one week before the Final.

Hopes that Jack Parr might make the Wembley team were always over-optimistic, however. There was talk about a special lightweight plaster cast being made so that he could play, but it was never a realistic option. The player was philosophical: "It's just one of those things, just bad luck. What really matters is that Derby County field the strongest available side and win the Cup. We shall reach the Final again, and then I'll get my chance to play." Charlton had also suffered a major blow when, ten days before the Final, their right-back, Peter Croker, fractured his right leg in a game at Tottenham. His was a desperately unlucky accident: with no other player near him he had slipped on the turf and caught his foot against a low wooden barrier.

On Good Friday, 19 April, there was some good news for Derby County – Woodley returned in goal for the visit of Arsenal. George Male put through his own goal to give the Rams a 1-1 draw before a Baseball Ground crowd of 28,156. Straight after the game, Stuart McMillan left for London. The team accompanied by trainer Dave Willis, secretary Jack Catterall and a director, left the Midland Hotel by motor coach the following morning, Easter Saturday, bound for The Valley and a Cup Final "rehearsal" against Charlton Athletic that afternoon.

McMillan made several changes from the team that had drawn with Arsenal. Sammy Crooks came back into the side at outside-right in place of Reg Harrison who moved inside to replace Carter. Stamps switched to inside-left in place of Doherty, with Dave McCulloch wearing the number-nine shirt. Dally Duncan was also missing, his place take by Angus Morrison. Charlton fielded a similarly cloak-and-dagger side as the *Derby Evening Telegraph's* Charles Mann reported:

"After Saturday's 'utility quality' Cup rehearsal at The Valley ground in which Charlton beat Derby County 2-1, only an astrologer would dare predict the result of the Wembley game – and he would probably be as far off the mark as astrologers usually are.

"My crystal ball being a bit clouded these days in consequence of the Rams having enveloped themselves in a mist of mystery, I can merely grope around in the fog of a few clues.

"Why in the name of the Official Secrets Act Derby County should suddenly take on a sort of 'cloak and dagger' of conspiracy is not one of the riddles I aim at solving. After all, it is the Cup they are trying to win, not an attempt to steal the Crown jewels.

"Both sides had a filleted appearance on Saturday. The 50,000 people who turned up to see what they thought would be a full dress rehearsal groaned loudly when the teams were announced."

Stamps earned Derby a half-time lead, but two goals from Charlie Revell, who would move to the Baseball Ground in 1951, gave Charlton a victory that may, or may not, have boosted their morale. Given the make-up of the teams it was difficult to tell.

On Easter Monday, 22 April, the Rams beat Arsenal 1-0 at Highbury, and then the players on the fringes of selection held their breath. Carter and Doherty had returned, and Harrison was back at outside-right. It seemed that Stuart McMillan was taking no chances and that it was young Reg Harrison who would take the number-seven shirt at Wembley. Sammy Crooks's illustrious career would not be capped by the dream that every footballer holds dearest from the moment he first kicks a ball.

The Rams winner at Highbury had astonished Charles Mann: "Stamps's goal, scored after half an hour's play, was an unusual effort. The play that led up to it was straightforward enough – a Carter-Doherty move, a fine pass by the latter to Harrison, and a nice centre – but I have never seen anything quite like the way Stamps balanced the ball on his head for several seconds before nodding it past Swindin [who had gusted for the Rams during the war]. A circus sea-lion could not have done it better!"

Mann put down this fine Rams performance to one thing – the return of Carter and Doherty: "The individual quality of these two craftsmen often dazzles people into missing their team-value. They dovetail into the fabric of the side like essential joints in a well-made piece of furniture."

The Rams party then headed back to their "secret" location – a hotel in Harpenden, Hertfordshire – from where McMillan had planned the rest of their week which included light training at Luton Town's ground, a visit to see Jack Buchanan in *Fine Feathers* at the Prince of Wales Theatre, an appearance at a football match between the National Children's Home and the Eagle Boys' Club of Harrow where they were introduced to both teams, an ice-hockey match at the Empire Pool, and, on the eve of the Final, an inspection of the Empire Stadium itself. For the moment, however, the Rams manager simply wanted to relax his players: He told reporters: "As far as the players are concerned, there is no such place as Wembley. We are just not thinking about it."

Derby County supporters were thinking about it. The Trix Novelty Company of Rutland Street, Leicester, had advertised "Derby County cardboard hats, attractive design in black and white with cockade and 'Derby County' on front. 36s per gross including purchase tax." Many of these were pressed into service on Saturday, 27 April 1946, when 12,000 of those fans, most travelling by train – 13 specials had been added to the regular Derby LMS-St Pancras services – descended on London for the FA Cup Final.

Arriving in the capital as early as 4am, many of them took the opportunity to enjoy a little sightseeing. In Piccadilly Circus and Leicester Square "the knots of two and three, and five and ten, leaned against buildings or stood on the kerbs viewing the London scene. Coventry Street adjoining the Circus and the Square was a 'Little Derby'". In front of Buckingham Palace, a group of men dressed in black and white asked if the King was at home. Even the crater in St James's Park where "Annie" – a 1,000lb German bomb – had been exploded the previous evening attracted its quota of curious Derby County supporters.

For many it was an entirely new experience. A father and son from Chaddesden, Mr A. J. Trueman and Mr J. W. Trueman, who lived next door to each other in Wollaton Road, were ready for breakfast after a walk that had taken in St Paul's Cathedral, the Embankment, the Houses of Parliament, Westminster Abbey, Hyde Park and Oxford Street. It was Mr Trueman senior's first visit to London. "It's very nice for a change," he told a reporter. Another small group of Derby fans said that they had queued outside a restaurant for nearly three-quarters of an hour – and then found only toast to eat.

There was a considerable street corner black market in tickets. One reporter said: "I watched a man wearing Derby favours sell a spare 3s 6d ticket to an unofficial programme seller for 30s. Fifteen minutes later the same ticket was sold for £3."

He continued: "Two Derby supporters to whom I spoke told me that they had travelled to London the previous evening and had spent most of the night walking about. All they wanted at the moment was a place in which to revive their energies for the match.

"Down the Mall I followed a steady tide of black and white into Trafalgar Square. Nelson always proves popular with visitors and only the fact that the first of the scaffolding ladders at the top of the column had been removed prevented a number of enthusiastic supporters from visiting him. One Derby man swore that he could see a black and white rosette pinned to Nelson's tunic!"

April 27, 1946

PICTURE
POST

DERBY COUNTY TAKES THE FIELD

The Rams make the front cover of Picture Post *magazine Jack Nicholas leads them out followed by Reg Harrison.*

The Rams FA Cup squad as seen by Derby Evening Telegraph *cartoonist "Sam".*

Rams fans outside St Pancras railway station on Cup Final morning.

The Rams party at their hotel at Harpenden in Hertfordshire, where they were based before the 1946 FA Cup Final.

WEST STANDING ENCLOSURE

ENTER AT TURNSTILES
(See Plan on back)

ENTRANCE

H 58

EMPIRE STADIUM, WEMBLEY

THE FOOTBALL ASSOCIATION
CUP COMPETITION

FINAL TIE

SATURDAY, APRIL 27th, 1946
Kick-off 3 p.m.

Price 3/6
(Including Tax)

MANAGING DIRECTOR,
Wembley Stadium Limited

THIS PORTION TO BE RETAINED
(See Conditions on back)

A coveted Cup Final ticket

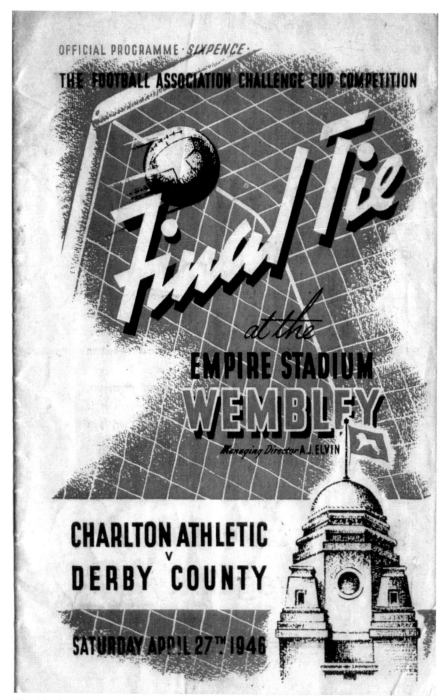

The 1946 FA Cup Final programme

A Curse Is Lifted

DURING the Second World War the FA Cup had enjoyed a lucky escape. It had been stored in a Portsmouth bank – Pompey being the last pre-war winners – but on the night the bank received a direct hit during an air-raid on the naval town, the club's manager, Jack Tinn, was sheltering under his stairs at home with the trophy clutched between his legs. In 1945, Portsmouth at last had to defend the Cup on the football pitch. They released their grip on the trophy immediately, losing to the only goal – which Reg Flewin put in his own net – of the two-game tie against Birmingham City in the third round. In the same round that saw the Rams beat Luton Town 9-0 on aggregate, Charlton Athletic were 4-3 aggregate victors over Fulham. That would earn them a unique place in the history of the

FA Cup by becoming the first club to lose a match in an early round but still proceed to the Final: they lost 2-1 to Fulham but still emerged winners of the overall tie.

Derby would have only four of their pre-war team on duty at Wembley – their captain, Jack Nicholas, Jack Howe, Dunkirk veteran Jack Stamps, and Dally Duncan – while Charlton Athletic, could call up six: Sam Bartram, who had been stationed at Alvaston in the RAF after war broke out; John Shreeve; Bert Turner; John Oakes; "Sailor" Brown; and Don Welsh. On Charlton's left wing was a player called Chris Duffy, a 27-year-old Scot, who had been discharged from army service after D-Day, suffering from shock. In the Cup run, Duffy became a regular scorer, including a hat-trick against Preston North End at The Valley on a gloomy Wednesday afternoon in February. It was only in the semi-final, however, that he finally caught the attention of the national newspapers. Against Bolton Wanderers at neutral Villa Park, Duffy had put Charlton ahead ten minutes before half-time, but it was his second goal, five minutes into the second half, which made the occupants of the press box sit up. It came at the end of a 35-yard run in which he skipped over or round the tackles of at least five opponents before shooting past goalkeeper Stan Hanson, one of 13 Bolton players to be involved in the retreat from Dunkirk. In the press room after the game, reporters wanted to know all about Duffy, starting, remarkably enough, with his forename; he was that unknown. The Charlton manager, Jimmy Seed, himself the veteran of a German gas attack in the First World War, was happy to fill in the details, including the fact that Duffy was recovering from a cartilage operation on his right knee, which meant that, all through that mazy run, he had been trying to manoeuvre the ball on to his left foot. It was the stuff of headlines and Duffy was the subject of plenty of those on the following day's back pages.

There was another newspaper story. In the week leading up to the Cup Final, an enterprising journalist, with an eye for a good tale, took Jack Nicholas to a gypsy encampment on the outskirts of London. In 1895, so the story went, Derby County had removed some gypsies from land that was to become the Baseball Ground, the club's home for the next 100 years. The gypsies had cursed Derby never to win a major football honour and, indeed, they had subsequently failed in three FA Cup Finals – one by a record defeat – and had never won the League championship. Palms were crossed with silver, the curse was lifted, and the reporter had his story (the gypsy later forecast a 3-2 win for the Rams and said that, anyway, a curse lasts for only seven years).

But would Derby soon have the FA Cup? First there was a threatened players' strike to overcome. The Derby players were furious that their wives had been given cheaper stand tickets than those allocated to directors' wives. Led by senior players, Doherty, Carter and Nicholas, they told the club chairman, Ben Robshaw: "No decent tickets, no game." Until the day he died, Carter was adamant that the 1946 FA Cup final would not have gone ahead if the Derby directors had not relented: "It was an insult, the directors' wives sitting under cover right near the Royal Box and our wives out in the open." Doherty, ever ready to fight an injustice, agreed: "There had been problems with tickets right from the start. Instead of getting reserved seats for friends, we were given cheap standing tickets. Then, on the Thursday before the Final, we each received a half-guinea ticket for our wife or nearest relative. We protested, asking for covered seats. The club said it was nothing to do with them; the FA had allocated the tickets. We stuck to our guns and two hours later, we each received guinea or two-guinea seats. In the end it was a storm in a teacup and was soon resolved. But we wouldn't have played and it showed how petty clubs could be towards their players just after the war."

For the first time in an English domestic game, linesmen would use luminous flags. The *Derby Evening Telegraph* reported: "The flags, of shiny peach and flame-coloured fabric, can be seen clearly in poor light. The original pair came from Burma where they had been used on an RAF airstrip for signalling to aeroplanes landing and taking off … when supplies of the material become available it is likely that they will be used for all big matches."

A Glorious Finale

"I KNEW we'd win the Cup because Raich said we would. When we arrived at Wembley, he just looked at us and said: 'Cup winners in town.'" So Reg Harrison summed up the confidence that oozed from the Rams camp in the days leading up to the 1946 FA Cup Final. Harrison and wing-half Jim Bullions, both in their early 20s, were the youngest players in the Wembley game that became known as the "Veterans' Final".

More than half the players were over 30. Charlton Athletic skipper John Oakes was 42, the oldest man ever to play in a Wembley Final.

Charlton were no strangers to Wembley. They had been there twice in the previous three seasons, losing the 1943 League South Final, 7-1 to Arsenal, and beating Chelsea

3-1 in the 1945 match. They were still favourites to win the Football League South championship in 1946.

The teams emerged from the Wembley tunnel into the brightness of a gloriously warm, sunny late spring day before a crowd of 98,215, who had paid a total of £45,000 in entrance money. The atmosphere was charged with emotion, tears rolling down the cheeks of hardened men during the singing of the traditional FA Cup Final anthem, *Abide With Me*. For all that had happened since VE Day and VJ Day, this was the first true indication that things were returning to normal after six years of war: the FA Cup Final was about to kick-off again.

The tension gripped the younger players especially and Bullions recalls: "My tongue was like a piece of dry leather." Charlton waited to be introduced to King George VI, who, despite the warm day, was wearing a grey overcoat. Queen Elizabeth and the two princesses, Elizabeth and Margaret, watched from the stand. First it was Derby's turn, their boots repaired with sticky tape, some of the numbers on their less-than-white shirts fraying at the edges, a sign of the austere post-war days to come. A month earlier there had been a rather mournful appeal in the Charlton match programme: "We are collecting coupons for kit. Can anybody help us?"

The Rams drew the number-one dressing-room at Wembley. "A lucky omen for me," said Raich Carter, "because it was the same one I had with Sunderland when we won the Cup in 1937." In fact, Carter was unaware that, shortly before the kick-off, his father-in-law had died. At his mother-in-law's suggestion, the news was kept from him and his wife until after the game.

The 1946 FA Cup Final was one of the best of all-time. "One of the most classic displays of football that Wembley has ever staged," wrote the great Alex James. For the first 80 minutes there was no score. "It was just like a normal First Division match," said Jack Howe. The Rams enjoyed a slight edge, though, and Carter claims that he was never in any doubt that they would win.

In the 80th minute Derby broke the deadlock, or at least it was broken for them by Charlton half-back Bert Turner. Carter took up the story: "I took three throw-ins in quick succession, the last of which I threw to Reg Harrison. He turned the ball to Jackie Stamps and he lifted it to Peter Doherty, who flicked it on with his head to where Dally Duncan tried a shot about ten yards out. Bert Turner tried to intercept it but somehow managed to divert it past Sam Bartram and we were in front."

In the crowd Jack Parr and Sammy Crooks were perched precariously on a plank when the Rams went ahead. Crooks leapt to his feet and deposited Parr, broken arm and all, on the ground. Derby's joy was short-lived, however. Two minutes later Bert Turner took a free-kick and the ball smacked against Doherty's right shin before flying into the Rams' net. Turner, who 30 years later was scouting for the Rams, is eternally credited with being the first man to score for both sides in an FA Cup Final. Yet Peter Doherty disagreed: "It was definitely an own-goal. If the ball had not been diverted off me, then Vic Woodley would have saved it easily."

The 1946 FA Cup Final thus went into extra-time. Yet even in the last five minutes it could have been sewn-up by Derby, had the ball not burst on the way to the Charlton net.

Jack Stamps's shot never got that far, "The bloody thing just went 'phut,'" said Jack, and Charlton were saved. Twenty-four hours earlier Cumberland referee Mr E.D. Smith, when asked the question on radio, put the chances of that happening as "millions to one". It is hard to understand why he would have laid those odds. Footballs were bursting all over the place. Two of Charlton's recent League South matches had to be resumed with a new ball. The league game between Charlton and Derby on the Wednesday after the Final would see another burst ball. And when Charlton returned to Wembley to meet Burnley in the 1947 FA Cup Final, the ball burst yet again. The Japanese invasion of Malaya in 1941 had meant that rubber was a rare commodity and better spent on things like aircraft production. Good footballs were simply in short supply at the end of the war.

Incidentally, Raich Carter had a low opinion of Mr Smith's performance in this match: "If anyone was overawed by the occasion, it was the referee. He changed his decisions several times. It was understandable, I suppose, because he was so far behind with play. If we had had a fast-moving referee, like the one in the semi-final, then we might have scored in the first half. Peter Doherty was brought down in their penalty-area, but when we looked around for the ref, he was too far behind play to give a decision."

With two minutes of extra-time played, the Rams went ahead without any argument. Stamps worked the ball down the left flank before cracking in a shot-cum-centre which Sam Bartram could only parry. The ball rolled loose and Doherty literally bowled Dally Duncan out of the way in order to slide the ball into an unguarded net.

Ten minutes later, Doherty returned the compliment and Stamps took his pass and went around Oakes and Phipps before scoring with a brilliant solo effort. A few seconds after the start of the second period of extra-time, Doherty's pass was again accepted by Stamps and the burly centre-forward put the issue beyond all doubt.

Alex James summed up: "The 1946 FA Cup Final was a memorable game with a glorious finale. Derby County's victory was complete and magnificent."

Saturday, 27 April 1946, Final (at Empire Stadium, Wembley)

Derby County 4 *Stamps (2), Doherty, H.Turner (og)*

Charlton Athletic 1 *H.Turner*
(after extra-time)

Derby County: Woodley; Nicholas, Howe; Bullions, Leuty, Musson; Harrison, Carter, Stamps, Doherty, Duncan

Charlton Athletic: Bartram; Phipps, Shreeve; H.Turner, Oakes, Johnson; Fell, Brown, A.Turner, Welsh, Duffy

Referee: E. D. Smith (Whitehaven)
Attendance: 98,215

Jack Nicholas introduces Jack Howe to King George VI.

A section of the 98,000 Wembley crowd.

It's Raich Carter's turn to be introduced to the King.

The injured Jack Parr meets the King.

Jack Nicholas and Charlton's skipper, Don Welsh, with referee Mr E. D. Smith.

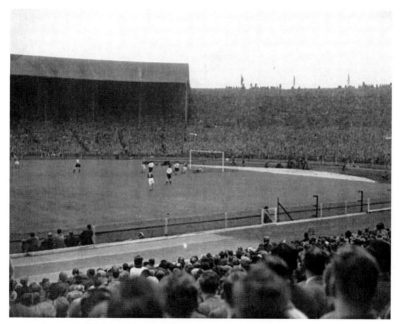

Crowd's-eye's view of the 1946 Wembley Final.

Dally Duncan watches as the ball beats Sam Bartram but goes wide.

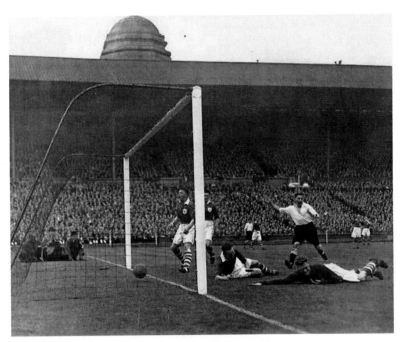

Delight as Bert Turner puts through his own goal.

Vic Woodley collects the ball as Leon Leuty holds off a Charlton attacker.

Sam Bartram, who was stationed in the RAF at Derby during the war, punches the ball away from Peter Doherty.

Vic Woodley punches clear from a Charlton attack.

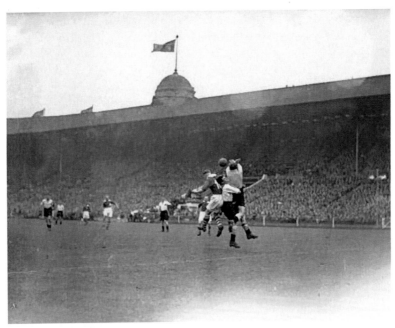

Woodley is again under pressure.

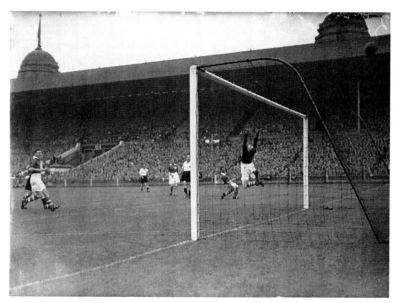

Sam Bartram tips the ball over the Charlton crossbar.

Charlton's John Shreeve clears up after a Rams attack.

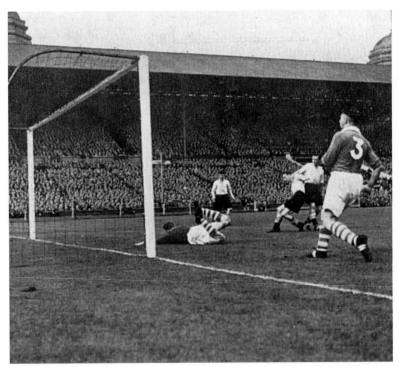

Peter Doherty knocks Dally Duncan out of the way and puts the Rams 2-1 ahead at Wembley.

Jack Stamps scores one of his two extra-time goals.

Rams skipper Jack Nicholas collects the FA Cup from King George VI.

Jack Nicholas with the FA Cup

The Rams players chair their skipper around the Wembley pitch, although young Reg Harrison can't take his eyes off his medal.

The Homecoming

O N Monday, 29 April 1946, Southampton greeted the FA Cup winners. Derby County still had three Football League South fixtures to fulfil, starting with a game at The Dell only 48 hours after they had walked out at Wembley. The Rams were without Raich Carter who had travelled back to Derby with his recently bereaved wife, and Dally Duncan and Chick Musson were also missing. Into Musson's place at left-half came Tim Ward, who had been given leave from the army just in time to take his seat at Wembley, while Stamps moved over to take Carter's place at inside-right with McCulloch leading the attack. Morrison stepped in at outside-left. The Saints were 2-0 ahead inside 11 minutes and although McCulloch and Stamps drew the Rams level, the home team scored twice more. The same evening, the Rams Reserves lost 5-0 on a Villa Park pitch which torrential rain had turned into a quagmire.

Twenty-four hours later there was to be no raining on Derby County's parade. Long before the team was due to arrive back home, thousands of people had gathered around the Blue Peter public house at Alvaston. Eventually, the Rams motor coach came into view and police had a difficult job in keeping back the thousands who swarmed towards it. The players transferred to an open-topped Offiler's eight-ton beer dray that had been decorated with black and white streamers, posters bearing slogans paying tribute to the team – and even a ram's head, supplied by a local butcher, on the cab in front.

Members of the Town Council, scheduled to follow the team into Derby aboard a Corporation double-decker bus, were dismayed to find themselves cut off from the main procession by a half-a-mile-long stream of traffic that infiltrated from side roads along the route into the centre of the town.

By the time the procession formed up at Midland Road, Derby's alderman and councillors were completely out of the picture and they did not arrive at the police station in Full Street until after the reception had started. Thousands of fans, most dressed in black and white, lined London Road as the procession, headed by mounted policemen and the Derby Borough Military Band, made its way towards The Spot. Patients at the Derbyshire Royal Infirmary were among those who threw black and white confetti at the parade, and the sea of humanity grew larger and larger as the procession edged its way down St Peter's Street, along the Cornmarket and through the Market Place.

Outside the police station – the Council House was only partially built and the Air Ministry had commandeered the usable bit – Jack Nicholas passed the Cup around to every member of the team who, in turn, held it aloft to new cheers from the throng. It was now proving impossible to manoeuvre the beer dray through a crowd now estimated at 20,000. So the players alighted and pushed their way through, led by Derby's chief constable, Colonel Horatio Rawlings.

From the police station balcony the players showed off the Cup again. The mayor told them: "It is no fluke that you have won the Cup, but by brilliant football throughout the rounds." After Ben Robshaw had addressed the crowd, Jack Nicholas introduced every member of the winning team as well as Sammy Crooks and Jack Parr. Each player said a few words, and Doherty, Carter and Crooks made longer speeches. Then the party returned into the police building where the Cup was filled with champagne as players, officials and wives celebrated.

The following evening, Wednesday, 1 May, the Rams met Charlton Athletic for the third time in 11 days, this time at the Baseball Ground in the return Football League South fixture. Charlton were still favourites for the title but a crowd of 30,000 saw the FA Cup paraded and the Wembley runners-up beaten, 3-1 with goals from Carter, Stamps and Doherty. Then members of both teams, minus Carter and Doherty, headed for the Grand Theatre in Babington Lane where they were guests of the management for the second house of a variety bill headlined by comedian George Doonan, with an adagio act – a cross between dance and acrobatics where the women were thrown, spun and swung around by the men – called the Ganjou Brothers and Juanita in second billing.

Charlton couldn't manage even second place. Their defeat at Derby left Harry Storer's Birmingham City to take the championship on goal average from Aston Villa. Charlton finished third, a point behind the top two, while a 1-1 draw against Chelsea at the Baseball Ground on 4 May saw the Rams finish in fourth place, five points behind Charlton.

FA Cup winners and fourth in the table – it hadn't been a bad season overall.

Derby County players show off the FA Cup after boarding an Offiler's beer dray at the Blue Peter, Alvaston.

The Rams parade down London Road and into Derby town centre.

The Cup comes down St Peter's Street.

The FA Cup procession passes Burton's the tailor's at the foot of St Peter's Street.

The FA Cup is shown off from the Police building in Full Street.

Raich Carter's FA Cup winner's medal.

Derby County, back at the Baseball Ground with the FA Cup: back row, left to right: Jack Parr, Jim Bullions, Jack Nicholas, Vic Woodley, Jack Howe, Chick Musson. Seated: Sammy Crooks, Jack Stamps, Stuart McMillan (manager), T. E. Wassell MBE (vice-chairman), Ben Robshaw (chairman), H. Walker (director), J. R. Cholerton (director), Peter Doherty, Raich Carter, Dave Willis (trainer). On ground: Reg Harrison, Dally Duncan.

Reluctant Tourists

RUMOUR had it that the Russians wanted to see the 1946 FA Cup winners. In the end, nothing came of that. Instead, the Rams arranged a tour to Czechoslovakia and Austria. Raich Carter was going to miss the Czech part of the trip. He had been selected to play for England in Paris and would join his Derby teammates in Vienna. But after the international, he received a telegram. He was to fly to Prague instead. It turned out that the Derby players had been expected to journey to Austria aboard army lorries rather than by air. The Derby directors refused, the Austria leg was cancelled, and instead, an extra game arranged in Prague, against a combined Sparta and Slavia team.

Derby had already lost 3-1 to Slavia and 3-2 to Sparta, but had beaten SK Zidenice of Brno, 2-1. All three matches had passed off without incident before crowds of more than 30,000. The only note of concern for the Rams players was that, before each game, girls in national costume presented them each with a huge bouquet of flowers. Floral bouquets and footballers have never quite gone together; in the ultra-masculine world of post-war Europe, 11 red-faced British footballers wondered what to do with them.

If anything had gone off in the previous games, then no-one has ever admitted it. But from the kick-off of this hastily arranged match, there was obvious bad blood, at least from the hosts who tore into the Derby players. They were well supported by some biased refereeing. Foul after foul went unpunished. Eventually, a Czech player held down Vic Woodley while his teammate rolled the ball into the net. The Rams players surrounded the referee, who indicated that he couldn't understand what they were saying, and the goal stood. Then Derby got the ball fairly in the net and, to their intense surprise, the goal was allowed to stand. Everyone in a white shirt had been expecting the referee to blow for an imaginary foul.

But it was ten minutes into the second half when the game really erupted. Scores of spectators rushed on to the pitch. They were after Peter Doherty, who had narrowly evaded a crude tackle and then watched as his would-be assailant overbalanced and took a tumble himself. The Czech reserves were first on to the pitch, closely followed by a section of the crowd. Carter looked to where he'd noticed a handful of British soldiers sitting. Alas, help was not forthcoming from that quarter, the squaddies, probably wisely, deciding that discretion was the better part of valour. Eventually, the local police sauntered on and calmed things down. Thankfully, no-one had been hurt, the protest more a lot of huffing and puffing and squaring-up than anyone actually laying a blow. None the less, Carter said afterwards that it was the worst game in which he'd ever played: "It was a good job that it was the last one of the tour because I'd have refused to play in another."

Back home, for cancelling the Austria leg of the trip the Rams faced the wrath of the Football Association. Worse still, the *Derby Evening Telegraph* carried letters from dozens of disappointed servicemen. Headlined "Troops Disappointed At Rams Fiasco", the newspaper reported that *The Eighth Army News* and *The Oak*, the organ of the 46th Division, had both devoted several column inches to the Rams' no-show.

The Eighth Army News had received a letter from Ben Robshaw, the Derby County chairman, who said that "owing to your altered arrangements without notice to us and the impracticality of travel to fit in with our other arrangements already made we were reluctantly compelled to cancel our tour to Austria".

"That sounds fair enough," commented the army newspaper, "but 30,000 soldiers who bought tickets for the Graz match will want to know just what are these altered arrangements and lack of travel facilities that make things impossible for Derby County to fulfil their engagements."

The paper said that a liaison officer had told it: "When shown the two troop carriers that were waiting outside the hotel to convey the Derby team on their hour-and-a-half journey into Austria, the Derby County chairman remarked that his men were not in the army. They were worth a lot of money and could not travel in that sort of transport. The troop carriers in question were fitted with padded seats and were the same type of vehicle that carried thousands of troops across Europe on land."

Seven members of a Parliamentary Delegation to Austria weighed-in, reporting how they had found thousands of servicemen "shocked that the manager and directors of Derby County F.C. had seen fit to break their pledge to play a game for the British troops in Austria", while typical of the many letters from individual soldiers was one from "Local" who said: "What excuse can I offer my comrades who are clamouring for Derby County's blood – who, like myself, have not, during the past three and a half years, been able to see first-class football – for being let down in such a manner by a team of heralded sportsmen?"

He continued: "Admittedly, army troop carriers are not of Mr Robshaw's standard, but they are considered by our boys of the Eighth Army as luxury travel on their five-day trip across Europe for leave. Anyway, I should like you folk at home to know how bitter a taste is left in the boys' mouths by my highly pedestall'd Derby County."

Riots on the pitch in Prague, the Eighth Army thoroughly cheesed-off – the trip had hardly been a roaring success for the new holders of the FA Cup.

The FA Cup holders are ready to fly off to Czechoslovakia in May 1946.

The Rams look a touch embarrassed as they are presented with bouquets of flowers before the start of their tour match against AC Sparta in Prague.

The Derby County party at Prague airport.

Rams players of 1946-47: back row (left to right): Jim Bullions, Bert Mozley, Alick Grant, Jack Howe, Chick Musson. Seated: Reg Harrison, Tim Ward, Leon Leuty, Angus Morrison, Jack Stamps, Ken Powell. That was the team that lost 2-0 at Villa Park in January. Inset are Frank Broome and Raich Carter.

Postscript

ON 11 January 1947, on a waterlogged pitch at Bournemouth, Derby County started their defence of the FA Cup.

It took the Rams only one minute to take the lead against their Third Division opponents, and the nature of the goal may have encouraged them to think that this was again going to be their season. It was, according to the *Derby Evening Telegraph* reporter Frank Nicklin, "the queerest goal I can ever remember".

Tim Ward was playing as a makeshift outside-left in place of Frank Broome, who had joined the Rams from Aston Villa in September 1946 but who was now nursing a pulled muscle. Nicklin described what happened: "Tim received the ball on the left wing, midway between halfway line and corner-flag and he banged it into the air almost haphazardly in the direction of the Bournemouth goal wishfully thinking, maybe, that some colleague might get his head to it.

"The look of incredulity which changed first to a grin of delight and then to a smirk of amusement when Bird, the Bournemouth goalkeeper, missed the ball as it bounced high and went over him into the goal, would have earned Ward a contract if he could reproduce it in a film test."

A few minutes later, Carter put the Rams 2-0 ahead. Bournemouth tried desperately hard to get back into the match – they hit the woodwork – but Derby held on. Nicklin was not impressed: "The freakishness about the rest of the game was that First Division Derby looked more like the popular conception of a Third Division side than did their Third Division opponents who enjoyed a remarkable revival and played a better class of football. The Bournemouth crowd, who expected big things from the Cup holders and would have considered defeat a fair price to pay for an exhibition of First Division football, went away moaning that Derby were poor value for the money."

The fourth round pitched the Rams against Chelsea at Stamford Bridge where they found themselves 2-1 down with only seconds remaining when Carter somehow got his hip to a loose ball and earned the Cup holders a replay. The return at the Baseball Ground was fairytale stuff. After only five minutes Alick Grant, the goalkeeper signed from Leicester City for £1,000 the previous November, dislocated his elbow and went on the left wing with Broome in goal, there being no substitutes allowed in those days. Broome did wonders, making one brilliant save from a Tommy Lawton header, and the game went into extra-time. Here it was the stuff of real boys' adventure stories. Grant set up a move in the fifth minute of the extra period. Harrison flicked the ball on to Stamps and the centre-forward struck the ball over Harry Medhurst's head for the winner. For years afterwards Broome would tease Lawton: "I'm the only goalkeeper you never scored against!"

In the fifth round the Rams faced Liverpool on an ice-bound Anfield pitch, across which there swept a bitterly cold wind – this was one of the worst winters in living memory and the football season was eventually extended to the beginning of June.

For three-quarters of the game the home side battered away at the Rams' defence. Woodley, back in goal, was magnificent. Frank Nicklin again: "The Rams' goalkeeper's safe handling and uncanny anticipation was reminiscent of the days just before the war when he was automatic choice for the England side. Throwing caution to the icy winds, Woodley displayed agility and, above all, great daring as he leaped and dived across the dangerous goalmouth surface."

The Rams held out until the 75th minute. Then Billy Liddell, "a certainty for the Great Britain XI to oppose the Rest of Europe at the end of the season" – sent in a harmless-looking cross from the left wing and Jack Balmer, who'd scored all Liverpool's goals when they'd won 4-1 at the Baseball Ground in November, came in from the other wing to meet the ball perfectly with his head and give Woodley no chance. That was how the score remained. Nicklin said that losing only 1-0 flattered the Rams. Whatever, their grip on the Cup had been released.

So, what happened to the team that won the FA Cup for Derby County? Given that, in April 1946, six members of that famous line-up were in their 30s, perhaps it isn't surprising that, within a very short space of time, five of them were no longer on Derby's books. Indeed, four of them didn't play in more than another season for the Rams.

Dally Duncan and Vic Woodley, who at 36 were the oldest members of the Cup-winning team, together with Jack Nicholas (35) and Peter Doherty (32), played their final Football League games for the Rams in 1946-47. Duncan made only two appearances before signing for Luton Town in October, and Nicholas nine, his last coming in a 3-0 defeat before 52,886 at Stamford Bridge in April.

Doherty played 15 times (and scored seven goals) and might have played for longer but for the fact that the Rams directors objected to his plan to take over the licence of the Arboretum Hotel. "I loved Derby," he told the author many years later, "but if those directors thought that me running a pub would be a problem for my football, then they didn't know me, and so I had no option but to leave. But I would have dearly loved to have carried on playing for Derby County and settling in the town." On Boxing Day, Doherty scored twice in a 5-1 win over Everton at the Baseball Ground and then completed his transfer to Huddersfield Town.

Goalkeeper Vic Woodley played 30 times in 1946-47. He appeared in the first 13 games before the Rams signed Alick Grant, but after Grant was injured against Chelsea in the FA Cup replay in January, Woodley returned and kept his place until the end of the season. Then he, too, left Derby and went back into semi-retirement with Bath City

With Tim Ward back from the army, Jim Bullions moved to Leeds United in 1947-48, and at the end of that season Raich Carter, who had been skippering the Rams, went off to become player-assistant manager of Hull City. He was 34 and looking to his future. His last appearance for the Rams was against Blackpool at the Baseball Ground and he marked it with the only goal of the game, his 50th in 83 peacetime appearances for the club.

In 1949-50, Jack Howe and Leon Leuty, both unsettled by the signing of Billy Steel, the precocious Scotland international who was favoured by the Rams board, moved, to Huddersfield Town and Bradford respectively.

Jack Stamps and Chick Musson played their last games for now-relegated Derby County in 1953-54. Stamps went to Shrewsbury Town, relative Football League newcomers, while Musson became player-manager of non-League Brush Sports.

That just left Reg Harrison as the last survivor of the Cup-winning team. He played his last game for the Rams in 1954-55, another relegation season. And then there were none.

Statistics and Players

Appearances
Bullions 11, Carter 11, Nicholas 11, Doherty 10, Leuty 10, Parr 10, Duncan 9, Musson 9, Stamps 8, Boulton 6, Harrison 6, Morrison 6, Crooks 5, Woodley 3, Howe 2, Townsend 2, Eggleston 1, Ward 1.

Goals (37)
Carter 12, Doherty 10, Stamps 9, Crooks 3, Harrison 1, Morrison 1, H. Turner (Charlton Athletic) own-goal.

Vic Woodley

Vic Woodley came into the Rams team for the semi-final after Stuart McMillan had signed him as an emergency measure following the injury to regular goalkeeper Frank Boulton. McMillan was certainly getting experience. Born at Cippenham in 1910, Woodley had been Chelsea's regular goalkeeper for most of the 1930s and had played in every one of England's last 19 internationals before the outbreak of war, and also appeared in two wartime internationals and for Chelsea in a wartime Wembley cup final. He was 36 and on loan to Southern League Bath City when the Rams negotiated with Chelsea for his release to play in the FA Cup. Woodley cost the Rams £1,000 and he soon repaid them with a brilliant save to deny Birmingham City's Harold Bodle in the Maine Road replay. Woodley remained at Derby, playing 30 games in the first post-war league season, before returning to Bath as player-manager. He died at Bradford-on-Avon in October 1978.

Jack Nicholas

Jack Nicholas had been with the Rams since 1927. When he signed from Swansea Town he already had a good Derby pedigree. He was born in the town in November 1910 when his father, also Jack, was the Rams' right-back. Nicholas senior moved to Swansea in August 1912, hence the connection, and Jack junior won schoolboy caps for Wales. But his heart was always with Derby. He started as a right-half and moved to full-back in the last pre-war season. In September 1941 he started a run of 328 out of a possible 331 League games to the end of 1938-39 and added three more in 1946-47. During the war he served as a policeman. He was primarily responsible for the Rams starting up again in 1941 and he captained the side that won the FA Cup. After ending his playing days he became the Rams' chief scout. He died in Nottingham in February 1977.

Jack Howe

Jack Howe was one of several North-East players signed by
George Jobey. Standing 6ft tall, he could kick equally well with
either foot. Howe was the Rams' regular left-back before the
Second World War, during which he served with the Cameron
Highlanders. He guested for Hearts, Falkirk, Aberdeen and
St Mirren, and represented the Scottish League against the
British Army. When the Rams' Cup run began he was on a
troopship coming home from India. He replaced the injured
Leuty at centre-half in the Maine Road replay and took Jack
Parr's place at left-back in the Final. When Raich Carter left
for Hull City in 1948, Howe became the Rams' skipper. He
won the first of three England caps in a 4-0 win in Turin in
May 1948. Howe moved to Huddersfield Town in October
1949 and played in non-League football until he was 40. He
died in his native Hartlepool in April 1987, aged 72.

Jim Bullions

Jim Bullions was born in Scotland in 1924 but came to Derbyshire as a 16-year-old to work in the wartime mining industry. He started his playing career with Clowne before signing as an amateur for Chesterfield in 1942. He turned down an offer from Blackpool in order to become a part-time professional at the Baseball Ground in October 1944, while still working down the pit. At 22 he was the youngest player in the 1946 FA Cup Final. He made 11 appearances at right-half in the Cup run but played in only 17 peacetime League games before the Rams let him go to Leeds United in November 1947, when Tim Ward had taken over the number-four shirt. Bullions helped Sammy Crooks establish Shrewsbury Town as a Football League club and later played and managed in Derbyshire non-League football. At the time of writing, with Reg Harrison he is one of only two survivors of the 1946 Final.

Leon Leuty

Leon Leuty was born in Meole Brace, Shrewsbury, in October 1920. He signed amateur forms for Derby County when he was 16 but also played for Derby Corinthians and Rolls-Royce, and guested for Notts County before becoming a professional at the Baseball Ground in May 1944. Leuty quickly established himself at centre-half – the great Tommy Lawton once nominated him as the best centre-half that he had ever faced – and only injury prevented him from being an ever-present in the Cup run in which he made 10 appearances. He went on to captain England "B" and played in the Bolton Disaster Fund international against Scotland at Maine Road, for which caps were not awarded. Unsettled by the arrival of Billy Steel, he moved to Bradford for £20,000 in March 1950. Six months later, Notts County paid £25,000 for him. He was only 35 when he died from leukaemia in Nottingham in December 1955.

Chick Musson

Chick Musson was another member of the Rams' Cup-winning team to die young. He was 34 when he passed away at Loughborough in April 1955, just a few months before Leon Leuty. Born in Kilburn in October 1920, Musson – given names Walter Urban – played for Holbrook St Michael's before the Rams signed him as an amateur in March 1936. He became a professional the following year but failed to break into a strong Derby team before the war. His chance came in 1944 and thereafter he was a regular, a powerful, hard-tackling wing-half feared by most opponents. He could play on either flank but it was as a left-half that he played in the Cup team, making nine appearances. He missed only five League games in the first five post-war seasons and played for the Football League against the Irish League in April 1950. He became player-manager of Brush Sports in 1954.

Reg Harrison

Reg Harrison was the other "baby" of the Cup-winning team. Born in Derby in May 1923, he played for Derby Corinthians before joining the Rams in March 1944. A direct, fast outside-right, despite his relative inexperience he was a fine replacement for the injured Sammy Crooks – "Reg never let me down," Crooks was still telling people 40 years later – and he made six appearances in the Cup run. Harrison was serving in the Royal Artillery and in inter-service matches he played with and against some of the greatest players in football and was never overshadowed. He scored 59 goals in 281 senior appearances for Derby. In 1955 he was one of six ex-Rams players in the Boston United team that scored a sensational 6-1 FA Cup victory at the Baseball Ground. He managed locally and still lives in Derby where he remains a popular figure, always ready to talk about the day that Derby won the Cup.

Raich Carter

Raich Carter was the Rams' leading scorer in the 1945-46 FA Cup with 12 goals from 11 matches. He was already one of the most famous players in the country with League championship and FA Cup winners' medals with Sunderland, and England caps to his name. He served in the fire brigade in Sunderland before joining the RAF, first at Innsworth Lane in Gloucestershire and then at Loughborough where he teamed up with Peter Doherty as they rehabilitated injured airmen. Carter guested for Derby County – his wife was living with her parents at Chaddesden – before signing for £6,000 in December 1945, just in time to play in the FA Cup. He later captained the Rams before joining Hull City in March 1948. As the Tigers' player-manager he helped them to the Third Division North title, and he later managed Leeds United, Mansfield Town and Middlesbrough. He died at Willerby, near Hull, in October 1994, aged 80.

Jack Stamps

"A rare battler" was how the 1946 FA Cup Final programme described Jack Stamps. Born in South Yorkshire in December 1918, he was given a free transfer by Mansfield Town in August 1938. His goals for New Brighton in the Third Division North persuaded George Jobey to pay £1,500 for him in January 1939. Two months later he scored twice on his League debut – against Charlton Athletic. Upon the outbreak of war Stamps joined the Royal Artillery and was one of the last members of the British Expeditionary Force to be evacuated from Dunkirk. In 1946 he scored nine goals in eight FA Cup ties, including two in the Final. Altogether he scored 126 goals in 262 senior games before joining Shrewsbury Town in December 1953. He later played for and managed Burton Albion. For the last 20 years of his life he was totally blind. He died at Burton upon Trent in November 1991.

Peter Doherty

Peter Doherty also signed for Derby in December 1945 after guesting for the Rams while serving at RAF Loughborough. Like Carter, he also cost £6,000 after falling out with his club, Manchester City with whom he won a League championship medal in 1937. Born at Magherafelt in June 1913, he played for Coleraine, Glentoran and Blackpool before City signed him in 1936. He scored five goals for the Rams against Aston Villa in the second leg of the 1945 Midland Cup Final, and ten goals in ten games in the FA Cup. Eight months after playing in the 1946 Final he moved to Huddersfield Town after the Rams denied his wish to take over the Arboretum Hotel. He managed Doncaster Rovers to the Third Division North title, and Northern Ireland to the 1958 World Cup finals. He won one of 16 caps for Northern Ireland while with Derby. He died at Poulton-le-Fylde in April 1990.

Dally Duncan

Douglas "Dally" Duncan joined the Rams from Hull City for £2,000 in 1932. His friendly rivalry with Sammy Crooks to be Derby's top-scoring winger was a great boost for the Rams for the remainder of the decade. Duncan also proved successful on the international stage with seven goals from his 14 appearances for Scotland – he was born in Aberdeen in 1909 – including both goals when England were beaten 2-0 at Hampden Park in 1935. When war was declared, Duncan went to the Carriage and Wagon Works on essential war work and played for their football team until the Rams resumed operations. Injury kept him out of the third-round tie against Luton but thereafter he was ever-present although he didn't manage to score a Cup goal. He had success managing Luton Town and Blackburn Rovers and was the Rams' choice to replace Tim Ward until someone suggested Brian Clough. He died in Brighton in January 1990.

Jack Parr

Jack Parr was one of a trio of unlucky Rams footballers who missed the 1946 FA Cup Final because of injury. Born in Derby in 1920, Parr played for Little Eaton St Peter's before joining the Rams as an amateur in December 1937. He became a professional three months later but was unable to break into a powerful Derby defence. But after the Rams resumed during the war he was a key member of the team at left-back. When Luton arrived for a league game on 3 April 1946, Parr had missed only two games all season (because he couldn't get time off work) but he fractured his right arm and it proved to be his final appearance of the season. He played for England "B" against the British Army in 1946-47. In 1953 he joined Sammy Crooks at Shrewsbury Town and ended his career in non-League football. He died in Derby in March 1985.

Frank Boulton

Frank Boulton cost Derby County £600 when they signed
him from Arsenal in August 1938. Born in Yate in 1917,
he had a trial with Bristol City before playing for Bath City,
from where Arsenal signed him in 1936. He played 15 times
when the Gunners won the League championship in 1937-
38. He was the Rams' regular goalkeeper in the final season
before the Second World War, during which he served with
the RAF in West Africa, and played in the first six FA Cup
matches of 1945-46 before being clattered by Swansea Town's
fiery centre-forward, Trevor Ford, in a league game. Boulton
returned briefly to the Rams' first team but was clearly still
troubled by the injury and he ended the season attempting to
recuperate in the Reserves. In July 1946 he signed for Swindon
Town and later played for Crystal Palace and Bedford Town.
He died in Swindon in June 1987.

Sammy Crooks

Sammy Crooks should have crowned his magnificent career with a place in the 1946 FA Cup-winning team. But he was injured in the second leg of the quarter-final tie against Aston Villa at the Baseball Ground when "Mush" Callaghan clattered him. Thereafter his role was that of chief morale-booster, a task for which his irrepressible personality was perfectly suited. Born in Bearpark in 1908, Crooks cost the Rams £300 when they signed him from Third Division North club Durham City in April 1927. He made 445 appearances and score 111 goals for the Rams, and played 26 times on England's right wing. Only Arsenal's Eddie Hapgood won more England caps between the wars. After that he managed several non-League clubs, took Shrewsbury Town into the Football League in 1950, and was chairman of the Players' Union. For seven years he served the Rams as chief scout. He died at Belper in February 1981.

Angus Morrison

Angus Morrison famously joined Derby County "for a box of cigars". That was the gift that Derby gave to the RAF officer who recommended Morrison to the Rams in 1944. Born in Dingwall in 1924, Morrison played for Ross County in the Highland League before joining the Rams. He was a good utility forward and excellent cover for the 1945-46 FA Cup team, playing in the first six games, either on the left wing or at centre-forward. He was unlucky not to play at Wembley, and, indeed, unlucky to play in an era when football was an 11-a-side game with no squads or substitutes. One of the players unsettled by the signing of Billy Steel, in November 1948 he was transferred to Preston, for £8,000, for whom he scored in the 1954 FA Cup Final. He played for Scotland "B" and later for Millwall and in non-League football. He died in Derby in December 2002.

Tim Ward

Tim Ward played in the first FA Cup game of 1945-46, the 6-0 win at Kenilworth Road, but was then recalled to the BAOR team that was entertaining British troops in occupied Germany. The next time he came on leave it was to sit in a Wembley stand and watch as his clubmates lifted the Cup. Ward didn't mind. Wounded on D-Day, he had seen friends killed, and he had been one of the first British soldiers to enter Belsen concentration camp. Missing a Cup Final was nothing by comparison. A stylish wing-half, born in Cheltenham in 1917, he joined the Rams from the local club in 1937 and soon established himself in the first team. In 1946 Derby turned down a £10,000 bid from Arsenal, and Ward went on to skipper the Rams and win two England caps. He later managed Barnsley, Grimsby, Derby and Carlisle. He died at Barton-under-Needwood in January 1993.

Bill Townsend

Bill Townsend was one of seven goalkeepers used by Derby County in 1945-46, and one of three who played for the Rams in the FA Cup that season. Born in Bedworth in 1922, Townsend played for Nuneaton Borough before joining Derby in the 1939 close season. His appearances in the 1945-46 quarter-final against Aston Villa were very much a baptism of fire because he had never before played for the Rams' first team in any kind of peacetime match. After the war he always seemed well down the pecking order and by the time he left for Burton Albion in July 1953 he had managed only 93 first-team appearances (14 of which had come in the FA Cup, incidentally). He later played for Banbury Spencer and returned to Burton as player-manager before posts as groundsman with Fylde RFC and sales manager with Everton's development office. He died at Thornton Cleveleys in December 1988.

Tommy Eggleston

Tommy Eggleston made one appearance for the Rams in the 1945-46 FA Cup, stepping in at left-half for Tim Ward in the third-round second-leg match against Luton Town at the Baseball Ground. After that, Chick Musson took over the number-six shirt. In fact was to be Eggleston's only peacetime game for Derby County, the club he had joined as an amateur in 1936. He turned professional the following year but was an eternal reserve before the war, in which he served as a Royal Naval petty officer. In July 1946 the Rams let him go to Leicester City and he was one of five Leicester players who signed simultaneously for Watford in January 1948. He played 186 times for Watford and became a highly respected trainer, coach, manager and physiotherapist both in England and in Greece. He was born in County Durham in 1920 and died in North Yorkshire in January 2004.